Secret Techniques
of
WING CHUN KUNG FU
(Third Level: Bil Jee)

K. T. Chao & J. E. Weakland

Paul H. Crompton Ltd.
94 Felsham Road,
London SW15 1DQ
England

1st edition 1983

By same authors:
**Secret Techniques of Wing Chun Kung Fu
First Level — Sil Lim Tao**

**Secret Techniques of Wing Chun Kung Fu
Second Level — Chum Kil**

ISBN 978-0-901764-62-1

Contents

Although there is nothing mystical about Wing Chun, as in other Kung Fu systems, it incorporates the ancient Chinese philosophical principles of Yin and Yang with all of their paradoxes. The cosmology is based on the "Book of Changes" (I-Ching) which views the universe as one great unity — a unity of opposites. Yin is the dark half of the circle and represents the feminine and the negative, while Yang, the white half of the circle, symbolises the masculine and positive. Yet there is a small white circle in the black portion and a small black circle within the white sector.

Preface

With the burning of the Shaolin monastery by the Manchus in the eighteenth century, the so-called Venerable Five scattered, and among them was Ng Mui, a Buddhist nun who possessed great boxing skills. Since the Manchus had gained a knowledge of Shaolin temple boxing from renegade monks, new techniques had to be developed. According to one story, Ng Mui devised her new system while observing a fight between a fox (or a snake) and a crane. These novel techniques were passed on to a young girl called Yim Wing Chun, after whom the style is named. From her the line of masters led eventually to Yip Man who died in 1972. This traditional history is recounted in the first chapter of this volume. The existence of the Venerable Five including Ng Mui, the truth of the story about the fox and the crane, and even the existence of Yim Wing Chun herself, can never be verified historically. But it would be a mistake to discount entirely the traditional history, for there is often a great deal of truth even in legends. It is important for students and practitioners of Wing Chun to keep before them the traditions of the system. As Yip Man has written, "A man will always think of the source of the water when he is drinking it."

The tradition concerning the connection between Wing Chun and Shaolin is too strong and too deep to dismiss, and this tradition places Wing Chun Kung Fu within the mainstream of the ancient Chinese world view as that view was shaped by the interaction of the three great religio-philosophical systems of Confucianism, Taoism, and Buddhism. Every serious student of Wing Chun should learn as much as possible about those three profound systems, for the present is rooted in the past. The deeper into the earth the roots of a tree reach, the stronger will be the tree; so it is with a person. The psychologist Rollo May is entirely correct when he says that the more profoundly a person can confront and experience the accumulated wealth in historical tradition, the more uniquely he can at the same time know and be himself. A knowledge of the techniques of Wing Chun must be coupled with an understanding of the Shaolin belief that training in the martial arts is for spiritual refinement in addition to self-defence. The ethic identified with the Shaolin Temple should always be kept in mind: "Learn the ways to preserve rather than destroy. Avoid rather than check; check rather than hurt; hurt rather than maim; maim rather than kill; for all life is precious, nor can any be replaced." In this regard the advice of Sun Tzu is worth pondering: "To win one hundred victories in one hundred battles is not the highest skill. To subdue the enemy without fighting is the highest skill".

3

The scholar John C. H. Wu has noted that the spirit of joy runs through Confucianism, Taoism, and Ch'an (Zen) Buddhism. Confucian joy springs from the love of learning, harmony of human relations, and the realisation of one's humanity. The Taoist joy consists in keeping oneself in tune and in harmony with Nature. The joy of Zen is found in seeing one's true nature. Common to all the three types of joy is the idea of harmony. Yip Man was deeply influenced by Confucianism and its principles of humanity, justice, propriety, and wisdom. There is within Confucianism the vision of the oneness of mankind. The Taoist vision goes beyond this and sees the oneness of the whole creation. There is considerable scholarly debate as to the existence of Bodhidharma, but tradition has linked his name to the reform of the Shaolin monastery and to the introduction of Ch'an (Zen) Buddhism into China. Ch'an is a branch of Mahayana Buddhism, but the Chinese modified the original ideas of this Indian school under the combined influence of Taoism and Confucianism. According to the Chinese Zen school, joy springs from seeing directly into your self-nature which means being enlightened and bringing enlightenment to others. This enlightenment comes in a flash, but you may prepare for it by meditation, discipline, and the cultivation of a moral life. It was a belief of the Shaolin Temple that the development of the mind could be achieved only after the body was disciplined. The monks were taught that a good soldier is not violent. A good fighter is not angry, and a good winner is not vengeful. Furthermore, they were taught to repay injury with justice and kindness always with kindness and that the one who conquers himself is the greatest warrior, a warrior at one with Nature, filled with compassion, wisdom, and the joy of self-knowledge; that is to say, enlightened. Such is the profound tradition of which Wing Chun is a part. These are the goals which you must keep in mind otherwise you will never transcend techniques to the point where the art becomes artless art. Keep before you the words of Chuang Tzu: "The mind of a perfect man is like a mirror. It grasps nothing. It expects nothing. It reflects but does not hold. Therefore, the perfect man can act without effort."

Shaolin and Wing Chun*

The Sungshan Peak is located in Honan. It is the highest of the Five Sacred Peaks and is known as the "Central Peak" of the five. Sungshan was already famous in the Ch'in (221-207 B.C.) and Han (206 B.C.-220 A.D.) dynasties. The area was looked upon as being the private garden of the emperors who lived in Loyang, their capital city not far away. There are over twenty peaks. The eastern parts are known as the T'aishih Mountains and the western as the Shaoshih Mountains. During the period of the Northern Wei dynasty, the Shaolin Temple was built. Dates for its founding vary. Some sources say 477 A.D. Others place it around 495-496 A.D.; one as late as 522 A.D. The Temple itself was surrounded by a forest of pines, thus the name "Shaolin" or "Young Forest," i.e., a forest of young trees. The word was appropriate in a symbolic sense, for a young tree can survive the violence of wind and storm because it bends and sways. "Therefore the stiff and unbending is the disciple of death. The gentle and yielding is the disciple of life" (Lao Tzu or Lao Tsu). Trees and people who are unbending are easily broken. The monks learned to bend, to yield, to flow in the face of the vicissitudes of life. They could say with Lao Tzu, "My religion is to think the unthinkable thought, to speak the ineffable word, to do the impossible deed, and to walk the impossible way." The monks of Shaolin needed resiliency because the monastery was destroyed and rebuilt many times through the course of its history. In the monastery were pictures of the five hundred legendary immortals of Buddhism. There was also the First Founder's Convent nearby commemorating Bodhidharma.

Assuming that Bodhidharma existed, and the great twentieth century scholar D. T. Suzuki among others accepts the existence of the great patriarch, this fierce looking monk arrived in Canton from India about 516 A.D. Then after a disastrous meeting with the emperor, journeyed north to Shaolin in 527 A.D. There according to tradition and legend he meditated for nine years facing a wall. So intense was his vigil that his shadow became part of the wall. Although he could have introduced some exercises for his monks, it is highly questionable that Bodhidharma was responsible for even inchoate versions of Shaolin chu'an. In fact even the book of exercises attributed to him was not published until over one thousand years after his death. His religious teachings were recorded during the Sui dynasty (581-601 A.D.) During that same period, one hundred acres of land was given to the monastery. In the early part of the T'ang dynasty (623-906 A.D.), a monk named T'an Chung led a group of monks against a remaining general of the Sui dynasty. The truth of this is less important than the martial spirit associated with the monastery from earliest times. The emperor praised T'an

Chung, bestowed honours upon him, gave land to the other monks, plus a gift of an additional forty acres of land to Shaolin together with a water wheel.

During the Yüan (Mongol) dynasty between 1341 and 1368, a number of bandits were harassing the Shaolin Temple; and the monks were afraid. A man working in the kitchen told the monks not to be frightened, that he would defend them. He took a long pole and stood on top of one of the mountain peaks, and the terrified bandits withdrew. One of the astonished monks said that the goddess Ku'an Yin had changed and became the defender; so the monks made a portrait of the defender and imitated his long pole technique. Later, according to the same legend, another monk came to Shaolin who looked like the defender. He taught Buddhist scripture to a monk named Ts'ing Tang and the martial arts (long pole and boxing) to another monk by the name of Pien T'un. This latter monk helped to rescue people from the barbarian border lands of Kweichow and Yunnan, and because of his heroism the natives took him for a god. Between 1522 and 1566 while the Ming dynasty was still in power, Japanese pirates were marauding along the coast of China. A government official asked Shaolin monks for assistance. Yua Kung led a band of more than thirty brother monks. They painted their faces and further disguised themselves and routed the pirates by using long poles made of iron. In the latter part of the sixteenth century a treatise on the long pole was written. The author of the treatise claimed to have studied at Shaolin for ten years. He said that at the time there were no "military monks," i.e., those skilled in the martial arts, in China except those of the Shaolin Temple. The author stated further that the martial arts were taught at Shaolin only for defensive purposes in order to protect their religion and that the long pole and Buddhism went hand in hand. He claimed that many people had heard about the Temple and respected it, for the Shaolin martial arts were renowned. According to the same author, the long pole was more popular than boxing at Shaolin, but that the monks were beginning to practice chu'an in order to make boxing as famous as the long pole.

We shall never discover the origins of Shaolin boxing, but it seems that fighting techniques patterned after animal forms eventually became a basic part of monastic discipline. The movements helped the monks develop grace, self-control, speed, patience, and tenacity. From the crane they learned grace and self-control and developed energy. The snake taught suppleness, rhythmic endurance and proper breathing. The way of the tiger strengthened the bones, while the way of the leopard harnessed the power. And from the dragon, their spirits learned to ride the wind. Other

Notes

* This chapter is based largely upon manuscripts and printed sources in Chinese plus some Western materials in English, French, and German, all of which are found in the Wade Collection of the University of Cambridge. We have included the traditional accounts and legends because they are all part of the heritage of Wing Chun. We believe with R. H. Tawney that legends are apt to be as right in substance as they are wrong in detail. Transliteration of Chinese words is necessary for the Western reader, but any pronunciation based on romanization would still be unintelligible to one versed in Chinese. We have adhered as much as possible to the Wade-Giles method and as a result have stressed the Mandarin tonal dialect. Nevertheless there are many inconistencies. Where there are common alternative transliterations, we have placed them in parentheses next to our transcription.

1. There is evidence that the colour system used by the Japanese for graded belts was adopted from the eight-banner system of the Manchus.

2. In Yip Man's story of the origin of Wing Chun, he states that Shaolin was burned during the reign of K'ang Hsi, thus placing the destruction of the Temple in the late seventeenth century. His account differs from those of the secret societies in the number of survivors. He states that the monks and their disciples scattered and among the survivors were the Venerable Five of Shaolin. The names of his five also are different from those given in the histories of the secret societies.

3. Before a student graduated from the Shaolin Temple, he had to pass several examinations, one of which involved a demonstration of 108 movements on a wooden dummy. One student did not finish and left the Temple by a tunnel used for refuse rather than by way of the exit which had the dummy. He then told people that you had to pass an examination which involved 108 movements and a wooden dummy. This was construed to mean 108 dangerous obstacles, thus developed the legend of the fearful exit from Shaolin, only one of many legends associated with the order.

4. Based on internal evidence and the succession of Wing Chun Masters, the seventeenth century date which Yip Man gives in his account is too early.

5. In 1930 a visitor to a Shaolin monastery observed that the monks practised in the early morning because of this dating back to the eighteenth century.

6. Although the very existence of a monastery in Fukien is doubted by a number of authorities, some sources state that in 1768, one of the Venerable Five established another Shaolin Temple in Fukien.

7. One source says on White Crane Mountain in a place called the Green Temple. In his account, Yip Man says that Ng Mui took refuge at the White Crane Temple on the slopes of Mount Tai Leung.

8. In his story of Wing Chun, Yip Man states that the beauty of Yim Wing Chun attracted the attention of a local bully, who was trying to force her to marry him.

9. Some accounts say that Ng Mui devised the new system, including the wooden dummy movements. Other sources say that Wing Chun was taught traditional Shaolin movements which she organized into the system which bears her name. Accounts vary also in regard to the amount of time Ng Mui's instruction took — from six months to three years. Yip Man merely says that eventually, Wing Chun was able to master the techniques, then challenged and defeated the bully. He goes on to say that Ng Mui's parting words to Wing Chun were to uphold the principle of the system, to spread the glory of Kung Fu, and to assist in the overthrow of the Ch'ing dynasty.

10. Some sources say that Wah was offered the post of Chief Instructor to the Soldiers of the Eight Banners, but he refused.

Miscellaneous Principles and Maxims

1. In general the term "Kung Fu" refers to an achievement, to something meritorious, to an ability, and is identified with an expert or sage. In Cantonese the term was applied to boxing and to other martial arts. This is appropriate in the sense that the mastery of Kung Fu requires considerable time, energy, strength, and most of all determination — spirit, the proper mental attitude. The more accurate term for boxing in Mandarin Chinese is *Ch'uan shu*, while *Wu shu* is the term applied to all the martial arts. The movements of Wing Chun Kung Fu provide good exercise for the body. The benefits will become obvious even after a short time. Your energy, strength, and endurance will improve as will your circulation and general health. The practice of the movements can help prolong your life. Your increased energy and health will in turn give you more confidence, and this confidence (rooted in an inner serenity) will manifest itself in an outer peacefulness. The more proficient you become in the movements, the greater will be your understanding of Wing Chun as a subtle and scientific system of self defence.

2. Today too many students attempt to master weapons before they have learned how to box. Boxing is the mother of the martial arts. Advance one level at a time in Wing Chun (Sil Lim Tao, Chum Kil, and Bil Jee). Only after mastering the three levels of boxing and the wooden dummy should a student attempt to learn the movements for the 6½ point long pole and the butterfly knives, because the boxing techniques are basic to both the long pole and the knives. Remember the advice of Confucius in the *Analects*. "Do not be desirous to have things done quickly; do not look at small advantages. Desire to have things done quickly prevents their being done thoroughly. Looking at small advantages prevents great affairs from being accomplished."

3. On the first level (Sil Lim Tao) the correct form for each hand and arm movement is stressed. At first the student must be relaxed and perform each of the movements slowly. Speed comes later.

4. After the hand and arm movements of level one are mastered, the turning movements of level two (Chum Kil) are introduced. Use the strength of your whole body. Always maintain a distance sufficient enough to reach an opponent with a complete punch. Never let an opponent get out of reach of a punch or a kick. Measure the distance with your eyes. Watch the entire field with your eyes and not just one part of your opponent's body. Keep pursuing your opponent so that he cannot get set. Keep him off balance; crowd him.

5. Whether you are attacking or defending, all of your movements must be precise, accurate, and executed with speed.

6. The following qualities are essential. You must be stable (body balance and an alert, clear mind which is without fear) accurate, relentless, strong, and fast.

7. Hand movements are often divided between Yin and Yang — one becomes Yin - (hollow), the other Yang - (solid).

8. You must develop skill in changing combinations faster than your opponent can counter them.

9. You must practise with someone. If you are afraid to fight, then your techniques are not deep. You need to practice with a partner. Do not worry about winning or losing. The more you have mastered Wing Chun, the less you will fear, but you need to think, to understand your weak points, and to practice in order to correct your mistakes.

10. The punch is the main thing. If you have a good punch, the one punch is enough. Some old Kung Fu masters of other schools called certain punches "seal" punches because they left a mark on the body and also caused internal damage. The story is told about the Wing Chun master Leung Tsan and his contests with other masters in striking melons. The melons would roll about ten times, hit the wall and crack when the other masters hit them. When Leung Tsan hit the melon with an arrow punch, it only rolled about five times and stopped. Although the melon was not cracked, when it was opened the entire inside was damaged. Such is the internal damage possible with the refined force of Wing Chun punches. There is a saying in Wing Chun that when you hit a person by the time you hear the noise the person already will be falling. In a word, when you punch an opponent, he should fall.

11. In every movement of the third level (Bil Jee), you use your hands and entire body at the same time. You should move and turn while delivering punches. This injunction is especially critical in regard to Yin and Yang knife hands. Your hands in punching and your feet in kicking should move in rapid fire like a machine gun.

12. The most important movements on each level are repeated several times in the Sets (Sil Lim Tao, Chum Kil, and Bil Jee).

13. One can defeat many, and the weak can overcome the strong with Wing Chun.

14. In our three volumes, we have explained as clearly as possible the techniques of the pure Wing Chun system as taught by Yip Man. But you must use your own imagination as you react to each situation spontaneously rather than on the basis of memorised responses. Apply the principles of Wing Chun with flexibility.

15. Maxims from *On the Art of War* by Sun Tzu, the oldest military treatise in the world. The following maxims of Sun Tzu have been in some cases modified in order to apply them to Wing Chun in a more meaningful way.
  (1) Your impact should be like a grindstone dashed against an egg. This is accomplished by "the science of the hollow and the solid." Use your strong points to attack the weak points of your opponent. Then you will know how to use Yin and Yang.
  (2) "In all fighting, the direct tactic may be used for joining battle, but indirect tactics will be needed in order to secure victory." One must know when to use the hard and the soft.
  (3) "The skillful tactician may be likened to be a snake that is found in the Ch'ang mountains." In ancient China, a battle formation was likened to a snake. If an enemy attacked the tail, the head of the snake would strike. If an enemy attacked the head, the tail of the snake would strike. The lesson for the boxer is obvious.
  (4) "Let your rapidity be that of the wind, your compactness that of the forest." Remember the essential qualities of speed and stability.
  (5) In attacking "be like fire, in immovability like a mountain." This is similar to a maxim in Wing Chun to the effect that in the horse stance the body is like a mountain from which the hands move like lightning.

  (6) The following two principles of Sun Tzu are useful in thinking about the arrow punch. "Energy may be likened to the bending of a crossbow; decision, to the releasing of the trigger. The force is potential being stored up in the bent crossbow until released by the finger on the trigger."
  (7) In regard to Yin (soft, indirect) and Yang (hard, direct), these maxims of Sun Tzu are pertinent. "In battle, there are not more than two methods of attack — the direct and the indirect; yet these two in combination give rise to an endless series of manoeuvres. The direct and the indirect lead on to each other in turn. It is like moving in a circle — you never come to an end. Who can exhaust the possibilities of their combination? To ensure that your whole host may withstand the brunt of the enemy's attack and remain unshaken — this is accomplished by manoeuvres direct and indirect." "At first, then, exhibit the coyness of a maiden, until the enemy gives you an opening; afterwards emulate the rapidity of a running hare, and it will be too late for the enemy to oppose you."
  (8) In Wing Chun, you must be relentless in your attack. "The onset of troops is like the rush of a torrent which will even roll stones along in its course."
  (9) Keep in mind the essential qualities of accuracy, strength, and speed. "The quality of decision is like the well-timed swoop of a falcon which enables it to strike and destroy its victim. To be near the goal while the enemy is still far from it, to wait at ease while the enemy is toiling and struggling — this is the art of husbanding one's strength. Thus the energy developed by good fighting men is as the momentum of a round stone rolled down a mountain thousands of feet in height." So much on the subject of energy.
  (10) Use your strong points to attack the weak points of your opponent. "So in war, the way is to avoid what is strong and to strike at what is weak. You may advance and be absolutely irresistible, if you make for the enemy's weak points; you may retire and be safe from pursuit if your movements are more rapid than those of the enemy."
  (11) You must be alert and apply the principles of Wing Chun with flexibility. "Therefore, just as water retains no constant shape; so in warfare there are no constant conditions. So await the opportunity, and so act when the opportunity arrives. He who can modify his tactics in relation to his opponent and thereby succeed in winning, may be called a heaven-born captain."

CH'I

Virtually every system of Kung Fu is concerned with proper breathing and the development of Ch'i, and Wing Chun is no exception. There are two kinds of strength. The strength of the body is an outer strength which is obvious and which everyone has in varying degrees, but it fades with age and dissipates with illness. Then there is Ch'i, the inner strength, which everyone possesses, too, but it is infinitely more difficult to develop than outer strength. Once the inner strength has been acquired, however, it lasts through every season, through old age and beyond.

1. Flowing Breath

Fig. ii. From the basic I.R.A.S. bring your arms down, while opening your hands to form the leaf palm. Palms should face your body. At the completion of this downward sweep the arms should be crossed at the wrist, with the left over the right. Figs. iii and iv. Inhale while you raise your arms back to the basic position. Imagine the air entering the right nostril as you raise your arms and picture it flowing out of your left nostril as you lower your arms again. This completes one cycle. When you inhale again, imagine the air coming into the left nostril and leaving through the right nostril. Alternate for each cycle. Breathe slowly and silently. Keep your tongue on the roof of the mouth. Begin with 20 repetitions (10 for each nostril). The next day increase to 25 reps for each nostril, and maintain this number. *Under no circumstances should you go beyond 25 reps.* You may begin your workouts with this exercise, especially on those days when you are practising the Sil Lim Tao Set because the movements of the flowing breath exercise are the same as those which begin the Set. The movements are also the same as those for the double cultivating hand exercise described in volume one *(Secret Techniques of Wing Chun Kung Fu – Sil Lim Tao, pp. 12, 80-82; hereafter referred to as Sil Lim Tao).*

2. Internal Breathing – Tan Tien Training.

"All things are backed by the Shade (Yin) and faced by the Light (Yang), and harmonized by the immaterial Breath (Ch'i) *Tao Tê Ching.* In Kung Fu it is believed that refined force (Gin Lek) is released from the lower abdominal region about three inches below the navel (Tan Tien). Human spiritual forces (Ch'i) are summoned from this region. The following exercise is designed to develop Gin Lek. Maintain basic I.R.A.S. but make sure that your arms are relaxed in the fist back position. Place your tongue on the roof of your mouth, keep your lips closed, and breathe very slowly through the nose. Expand the abdomen while inhaling and contract it while exhaling, all the while concentrating on the Tan Tien, i.e., the lower abdominal region. Remember to inhale and to exhale slowly and silently. Breathing should be entirely abdominal. The upper portion of the chest and the rib cage should not be involved. In addition to the obvious benefits to the heart and lungs, this exercise will strengthen and tone the abdominal muscles. Do this exercise about 15 minutes each day. Divide the time by doing 5 minutes in the morning, 5 minutes during your Wing Chun session, and a final 5 minutes before going to bed. *Under no circumstances exceed the times mentioned. More is not better.*

In regard to these breathing exercises and in regard to exercise in general, consult your physician before embarking upon any regimen. The rhythmic breathing of Tan Tien training is soft and gentle, akin to meditation. "Empty yourself of everything. Let the mind rest at peace. The ten thousand things rise and fall while the Self watches their return. Returning to the source is stillness, which is the way of nature. The way of nature is unchanging. Being at one with the Tao is eternal" *(Tao Tê Ching)*.

i

iii

ii

iv

The Techniques of Bil Jee

Introduction

The third level of Wing Chun is called *Bil Jee,* which means "thrusting fingers," or "dart fingers." The maxim of the Wing Chun School was that Bil Jee should never go out of the door, i.e., this level was to remain secret. This level is seldom used, however, except against an advanced opponent. The repetitions and time segments recommended in this book and in the previous volumes are designed to duplicate the strenuous routines of the Yip

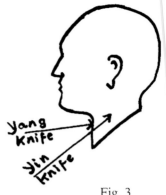

Fig. 3

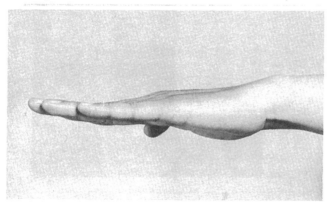

Fig. 1

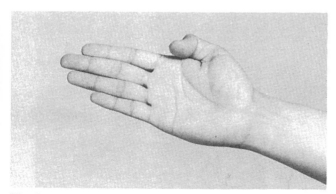

Fig. 2

Man School. This volume follows the pattern of the previous ones: movements are explained in full, exercises given, applications shown, numerous sparring sets depicted, and Bil Jee Set fully illustrated. This volume assumes that the reader is familiar with Levels 1 and 2; thus the basic techniques of the Sil Lim Tao and the Chum Kil are not explained again. You should not go on to level three until you have mastered the first two levels.

Figure 1 shows the arm in the yang knife hand position together with the points of contact. The striking surface of the yang knife hand is the edge of the hand. The outside of the forearm is used for blocking. Finally the finger tips are used for the dart fingers thrust, an important element in the third level, i.e., "thrusting fingers." See volume one for a complete description of the dart fingers thrust, which is delivered along the centreline into the eyes of an opponent (Sil Lim Tao, pp. 47-48). To avoid confusion, the dart fingers thrust will be called *bil jee sao* in order to distinguish it from the *Bil Jee* Set. The arm shown in figure 2 is in the yin knife hand position. The point of contact is the edge of the hand. Figure 3 illustrates by a diagram the areas of the neck and throat to which the yin and yang knife hands are directed.

18

Fig. 4

Fig. 4 ("L" refers to the person on the left, and "R" refers to the one on the right.) "R" delivers a right yin knife hand to the side of "L's" neck. Remember that the power is concentrated in the edge of the hand (*Sil Lim Tao*, pp. 54-57). Fig. 5. "R" delivers a right yang knife hand to the throat of "L". Practice the drop elbow block and yang knife hand exercise described in level one (*Sil Lim Tao*, p. 41).

Fig. 5

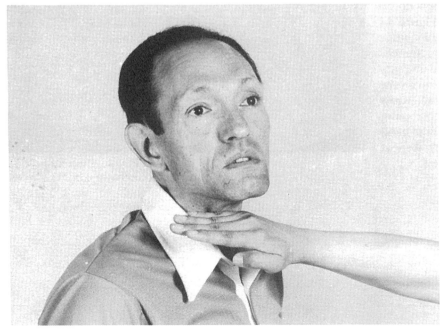

19

Wrist Exercise

Continue the wrist exercises described in level two, especially the one with the bottles *(Secret Techniques of Wing Chun Kung Fu. Second Level: Chum Kil,* p. 10; hereafter referred to as *Chum Kil).* To those exercises, add the following one. Figs. 6 (front view) and 7 (side view). From basic position execute a right arrow punch, and then open your fist to form a leaf palm. Fig. 8. Move the hand downward by means of a wrist motion (ulnar deviation). The hand will be on a diagonal, fingers straight and pointed toward the floor. Fig. 9. Return to position shown in figure 7. Then move the hand so that the palm is down. Fig. 10. By a movement of the wrist joint (radial deviation) turn the hand to the right. Repeat the movements shown in figures 7 – 10 for 50 reps. Return to the basic position, and then do 50 reps with the left hand. Figure 11 shows the fist opened after executing a left arrow punch. Figures 12 (front view) and 13 (side view) illustrate the downward movement (ulnar deviation), while figures 14 and 15 depict the palm down and the movement of the hand to the left (radial deviation). Repeat for 3 sets of 50 reps each hand.

6

7

11

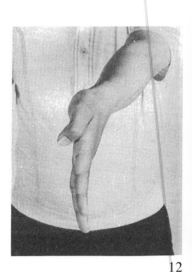

12

8

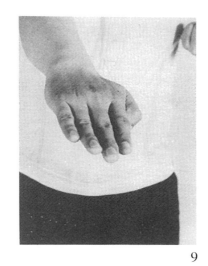

9

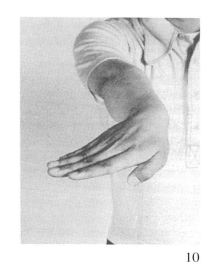

10

14

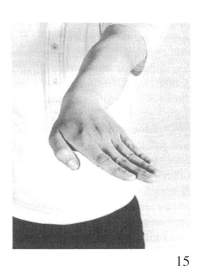

15

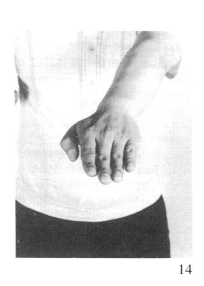

13

21

Bowing Down Elbow Punch with Protective Hand while Turning

The Chinese word for this punch means "to bow down" or "to kneel down" because of the motion of the elbow downward; thus we are calling it the "bowing down elbow punch." Hereafter this will be referred to as B.D.E.P. Contrast this with the parallel elbow punch (*Chum Kil*, pp. 38-80). You must use your entire body when delivering this punch. The shoulder does not move without the body. The bowing down elbow punch is especially effective when combined with a dart fingers attack (bil jee sao). In volume two, we spoke of three basic turns of 30°, 45°, and 90°; but these are just approximations. For example, in a 90° turn although the hips are turned 90° from the centre, the feet are only turned about 80°. In Wing Chun turns, the hips, knees and feet work in unison, i.e., pivot together as one (*Chum Kil*, pp. 24-36). This enables you to use the strength of your entire body. Likewise in delivering the bowing down elbow punch, use the force of your whole body against your opponent whether turning or moving forward, remember not to be off balance. Just as the wing hand moves with the entire body, so too does the bowing down elbow punch (*Chum Kil*, p.65). The bowing down elbow punch is executed as follows. In the basic position, relax your fists and shoulders. Turn while delivering the punch, using your entire body. The momentum

16   17

of your body will carry the elbow. Your hand should be close to the chest and the shoulder must be relaxed as in the wing hand. The problem is that your arm might be tense and you must relax it suddenly in order to execute the punch. There is a kind of upward movement of the elbow as in the wing hand, then the elbow moves forward and down. Remember that you never execute this punch without using the body either in turning or in moving forward.

1. **B.D.E.P. with protective hand while turning 90°.**
   Fig. 16. Assume the basic horse stance position. Relax fists and shoulders. Fig. 17. Execute a left bowing down elbow punch while turning 90° to the right of centre. At the same time move the right protective hand in position. Fig. 18. Then immediately deliver a right B.D.E.P. while turning 90° to the left of centre. Do 4 sets of 50 reps. each side. Figure 19 shows the right B.D.E.P. as seen straight ahead. In figure 20, "R" has delivered a right B.D.E.P. to "L's" centreline.

2. **B.D.E.P. with protective hand while turning 30°.**
   Fig. 21. From basic position (as shown in figure 16) execute a left B.D.E.P. and right protective hand while turning 30° to the right of centre. Fig. 22. Then deliver a right B.D.E.P. and left protective hand while turning 30° to the left of centre. Do 4 sets of 50 reps each side.

18

19

22

21

20

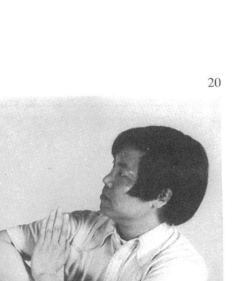

23

B.D.E.P. while Moving Forward

Review the directions for the sliding step given in level two (*Chum Kil*, pp. 63-66). Begin in the basic position (as shown in figure 16). Fig. 23. Take a left sliding step forward while executing a left B.D.E.P. and right protective hand. Return to the basic position. Then take a right sliding step forward while delivering a right B.D.E.P. and left protective hand. Do 4 sets of 50 reps each side.

Application

Fig. 24. "R" attempts a right arrow punch which "L" blocks with a left prayer palm. Fig. 25. "R" counters by changing the right arrow punch into a right B.D.E.P. while moving forward.

23

24   25

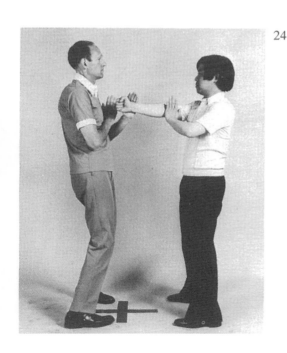

Flexibility Exercise for the B.D.E.P.

This exercise, which is a circular movement, is designed to develop flexibility. It also tones the shoulders, trapezius, serratus magnus and latissimus dorsi. Fig. 26. Touch your shoulder with your fingers, keeping elbows in front. Fig. 27. Raise the elbows while keeping them close together. Fig. 28. Move the elbows outward. Fig. 29. Finally move the elbows down. Repeat the entire sequence for five minutes; then relax.

26   27

 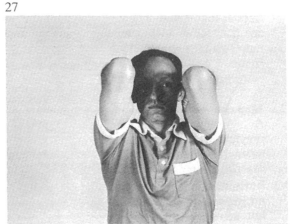

28   29

 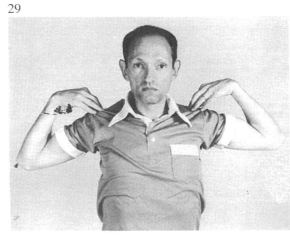

Snake Hand and Dart Fingers

1. Exercise

Review the directions, exercises, and sparring sets of level one dealing with the snake hand and dart fingers (*Sil Lim Tao,* pp. 45-51). In the exercise and sparring set for level three, you should concentrate on the outer forearm. Fig. 30. From the basic position, move your left hand into a snake hand position. Fig. 31. Then execute a left dart fingers attack (*bil jee sao*). Return to the snake hand position. Repeat for 50 reps. Then do the same with the right hand for 50 reps. In all do 3 sets of 50 reps with each hand.

2. Sparring Set.

As mentioned in previous volumes, partners switch about in sparring sets. Fig. 32. Both are in the basic position. "L" delivers a left arrow punch which "R" blocks with a left snake hand. Fig. 33. "L" then delivers a right arrow punch which "R" blocks with a left dart fingers thrust. Note that the point of contact is the outer forearm of "R". Repeat 25 times. Then shift hands, i.e., "L" begins by executing a right arrow punch which "R" blocks with a right snake hand, etc. for another 25 reps. Compare with the thrusting blocks of level one (*Sil Lim Tao,* p.53).

30   31

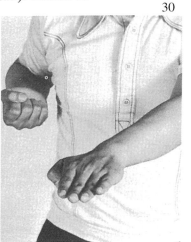 

32   33

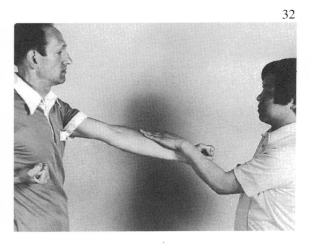 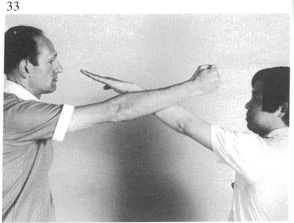

Semicircular Sliding Step

This is a very important movement because it keeps your opponent off balance.

1. Exercise

Fig. 34.

Begin in the horse stance (I.R.A.S.). Shift your weight to the right leg. Slide the left foot over to the right. Then make a semicircle while sliding the left foot back to the starting position.

Fig. 35

Then shift your weight to the left leg and slide the right foot over, etc. Alternate for 3 sets of 50 reps.

2. Semicircular sliding step forward.

This movement is very similar to the triangular step in level two (*Chum Kil*, pp. 68-72). The foot should glide lightly, quickly, and smoothly across the ground. The purpose of this particular charging stance is to knock your opponent off balance. In training you practice making a semicircle, but in combat a small circle might suffice. It depends upon the distance and position of your opponent.

Exercise.

Figs. 36a and 36b. Assume basic I.R.A.S. Shift weight to right leg. Slide left foot toward the right, and then move it forward in a semicircle. Shift weight to left leg while you slide the right forward as indicated in figure 36b, because the feet should remain equidistant from each other. Then the weight is shifted back to the right foot. Note that the left

36a

hand is inquisitive while the right one is protective. As noted in level two, the inquisitive hand and the front leg are same – in the case of fig. 36a, the left leg and the left hand. Figure 36a, shows the completion of the sliding step forward with the left foot.

Fig. 36b.

27

Figs. 37a and 37b. From the position in figure 36a, shift the weight slightly to the left leg, while you slide the right foot to the left. Then move it forward in a semicircle. Shift weight for a moment to the right leg, while you slide the left forward as indicated in figure 37b. Then the weight is shifted back to the left leg which is in the rear. Note that the right hand is now the inquisitive hand, while the left is now the protective one. Figure 37a, shows the completion of the sliding step forward with the right foot.

37a

Fig. 37b.

Practice going forward for 10 minutes.

Application.
Fig. 38. "L" has thrown a right arrow while in a charging stance with the right leg forward. "R" has executed a right semicircular sliding step forward and a right open hand block (crossed open hand block) which have knocked "L" off balance. In addition, "R" has delivered a sideward palm strike with his left hand to the ribs of "L". See level one for the sideward palm strike (*Sil Lim Tao,* pp. 54-56). For counter, see level two (*Chum Kil,* p.52, fig. 154).

38

28

B.D.E.P. with Yin Knife Hand and Sideward Palm Strike

1. **Yin knife hand exercise.**
   Fig. 39. Assume basic horse stance. Left hand should be in the inquisitive position with the right as protective. Fig. 40. Execute a left yin knife hand while turning 30° to the right of centre. Note that the right hand remains in the protective position. Fig. 41. Then execute a right yin knife hand while turning 30° to the left of centre. Note that the left hand becomes the protective one. Alternate for 2 sets of 50 reps.

39

2. **Application.**
   Fig. 42. "L" has delivered a left arrow punch which "R" has blocked with a left push down palm while at the same time "R" has executed a right yin knife to the neck of "L". In the beginning "R" was in an on guard position with the right hand as inquisitive and the left as protective.

40

41

42

3. B.D.E.P. and yin knife exercise.

Fig. 43. Begin in the basic horse stance. Execute a left B.D.E.P. while turning 30° to the right of centre. The right becomes the protective hand. Fig. 44. The right hand shifts under the left elbow. In fighting, you shift the hand immediately if the situation demands it; but for purposes of illustrating the exercise the movement has been divided. Fig. 45. Then you immediately deliver a right dart fingers thrust. Emphasis is on the forearm because it is a thrusting block. Fig. 46. The right dart fingers thrust retracts and becomes a snake hand, while the left B.D.E.P. changes to a yin knife hand to the neck. Then change the hand into a right B.D.E.P. while turning 30° to the left of centre. The left knife hand becomes the protective hand and moves under the right elbow. Then you immediately deliver a left dart fingers thrusting block. The left retracts and becomes a snake hand, while the right B.D.E.P. changes to a yin knife hand to the neck. Alternate for 50 reps each side. In all do 3 sets of 50 reps.

43

44

45

46

Application

47

48

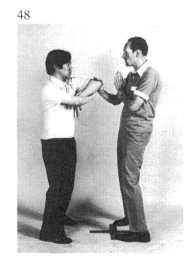

49

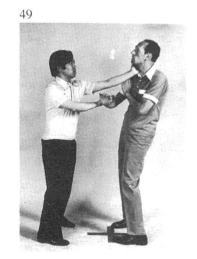

50

4. Application

Fig. 47. "L" begins a left B.D.E.P. while turning 30° to the right. The right hand is protective. "R" counters by using a right prayer palm with the left held in a protective position. Fig. 48. "L" moves right hand under the elbow in preparation for a right dart fingers thrusting block if necessary to counter a possible left arrow punch from "R". Fig. 49. It was not necessary for "L" to use a thrusting block; so the right becomes a snake hand which pulls "R's" right arm down while the left B.D.E.P. changes to a left yin knife hand to "R's" neck. *Note:* When moving the protective hand under the elbow of a B.D.E.P., you must do so rapidly otherwise it will be trapped. Never have it close to the body between the elbow and shoulder area. If so, your opponent can push your B.D.E.P. down and your elbow will trap your other hand as in figure 50 in which "L's" right hand is pinned by his own left elbow.

5. B.D.E.P. palm strike exercise.

Perform the same movements as described for figures 43-45, but execute a sideward palm strike with the left hand to the rib area while the right retracts to a snake hand as shown in figure 51. Then change the right snake hand into a right B.D.E.P. while turning 30°to the left of the centre. The left sideward palm becomes the protective hand and moves under the right elbow. Then you immediately deliver a left dart fingers thrusting block. The left retracts and becomes a snake hand, while the right B.D.E.P. changes to a right sideward palm strike to the ribs. Alternate for 50 reps each side. In all do 3 sets of 50 reps.

6. Application.

The movements are the same as shown in figure 47-48. Fig. 52. "R" uses a right snake hand which pulls "L's" right arm down while the left B.D.E.P. changes to a left sideward palm strike to the ribs. One can also execute a yin knife hand to the ribs. In that case the edge of the hand is the point of contact.

51

52

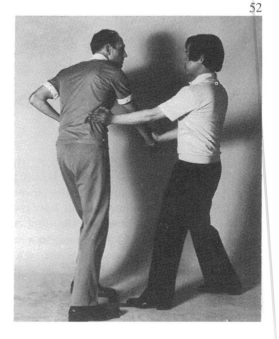

Jeet Sao

In Chinese, *jeet* means "to intercept" or "to obstruct," *sao* means "hand." We have, therefore, called this movement "obstructing hand." In volume two we used the term "intercepting hand" for the *lan sao* (*Chum Kil*, p.45). *Lan* really means "to retard," but we preferred the term "intercepting;" thus to avoid confusion, we have called the *jeet sao* "obstructing hand." The jeet sao is like a fac sao (Extended Hand, *Sil Lim Tao*, pp. 35-36; *Chum Kil*, p.46) and a gahng sao (Cultivating Hand, *Sil Lim Tao*, pp. 62-67). The jeet sao is executed with the inquisitive hand, (man sao) and is a powerful block. In a word, the man sao becomes a jeet sao. With it you can push an opponent's arm away. The contact point is the hard portion of the outside of the forearm.

53

1. **Execution of the jeet sao.**

   Fig. 53. This illustrates I.R.A.S. with left inquisitive and right protective. Fig. 54. The left inquisitive hand shoots forward and turns at the same time so that at the completion of the move the hand is in a reverse position with the palm facing to the left with the thumb down. The jeet sao is executed with the piston-like thrust of an arrow punch.

54

2. Exercise in preparation for the jeet sao.

Assume the position shown in figure 55. Without bending the elbows, circle the arms in a clockwise direction. Continue for 3 minutes. Rest and repeat for another 3 minutes.

3. Jeet sao exercise.

Begin in basic fist back I.R.A.S. position. Fig. 56. Execute a left jeet sao and right protective hand. Your head should turn to watch the left hand. Concentrate on the left forearm. Fig. 57. Then do a right jeet sao and a left protective hand. Your head should turn to watch the right hand. Concentrate on the right forearm. Even though your head is turned in this exercise to watch the jeet sao, by peripheral vision you should see the front too. This is

55

important because in combat you must see the whole field. Do 4 sets of 50 reps with each arm.

56

57

34

4.   Applications

58

59

60

Application number one.
Fig. 58. "R" delivers a left arrow punch. "L" blocks it with a left wing hand (a crossed wing hand) and the right is in a protective position. Fig. 59. "L's" right becomes a prayer palm which slaps aside "R's" left arrow. "L's" left wing changes to a jeet sao striking the ribs of "L" with the edge of the hand.

Application number two.
Fig. 60. "R" delivers a right arrow which "L" blocks with a left jeet sao. "L's" right hand is held in a protective position. Fig. 61. "L" moves forward with left leg and delivers a left yin knife hand to "R's" neck, i.e., "L's" jeet sao changes into a yin knife hand.

61

Application number three.

Fig. 62. "R" executes a right arrow to stomach of "L". But "L" blocks with a right jeet sao (a crossed jeet sao). Fig. 63. "L" moves forward with right leg in a semicircular step while the jeet sao changes to a sideward palm strike to the ribs of "R".

Application number four.

Fig. 64. "L" delivers a left arrow which "R" blocks with a right jeet sao. "R's" left hand is in protective position. Fig. 65. "R" steps forward while doing a lap sao, i.e., "R's" left pushes "L's" left arrow down while changing the jeet sao into a yang knife hand. Refer to the directions in levels one and two for lap sao (*Sil Lim Tao*, p.74; *Chum Kil*, pp. 48-53).

62

63

64

65

Candle Test

This test, introduced in level one, is, according to the traditional history, the ancient Shaolin method for the demonstration of refined force. What is the purpose of so difficult a test? "Discipline. That you may strike with such force, yet in one place and no other." Place a lighted candle in front of you at heart level. The candle should be a little over arm's length away from you so that your fist (palm or edge of hand) is about 1 to 2 inches from the candle. Then deliver a punch. The speed of it should put out the candle. When you are able to do this, you can be sure that the punch or strike is effective. Note that it is important not to touch the candle. This test will help you attain absolute control and accuracy. On the third level you should pay special attention to vertical palm strike (figure 66) and the yin knife hand (figure 67).

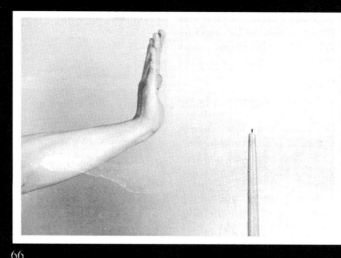

66

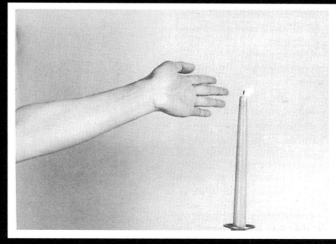

67

Shortened Punches

Shortened punches were introduced in level two (Chum Kil, pp. 7-8). In Wing Chun, punches of great power can be delivered from short distances. Shortened punches also can be used to catch an opponent who moves or evades your first punch.

1. Exercise.
   Fig. 68. Begin in a basic I.R.A.S. position. Execute a left arrow punch while turning 30° to the right of centre. Fig. 69. Then retract your left arm slightly, change to a yin knife hand, and immediately deliver a left yin knife hand while turning another 15°. Repeat 50 times. Then do the exercise with the right arm for another 50 reps. In all do 3 sets of 50 reps each arm.

2. Applications.
   Application number one.
   Fig. 70. "R" delivers a right arrow punch while turning 30° to the left of centre; but "L" slips the punch by moving his head to the right. Fig. 71. "R" retracts his right arm slightly, changes it to a yin knife hand, and immediately executes a right yin knife hand to the neck of "L" while turning another 15°.

68

69

70

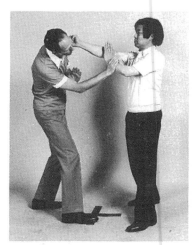

71

Application number two.
Fig. 72. "R" delivers a right dart fingers attack to eyes of "L", but "L" evades it by moving his head back. Fig. 73. "R" retracts right arm slightly and converts it to a vertical palm which "R" delivers to "L's" exposed chin, moving forward while striking the blow.

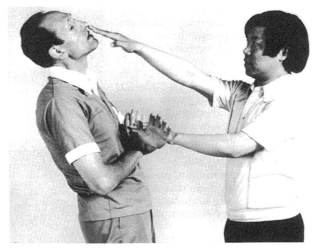

72

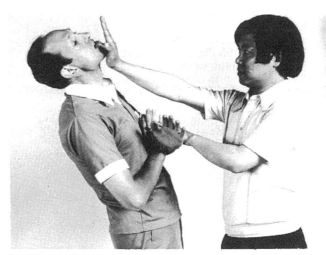

73

Push Down Palm and Yang Knife Hand.

1. Exercise number one.
   Fig. 74. Begin in basic position. Do a left push down palm. Fig. 75. The left push down palm changes to a left yang knife hand. Repeat 25 times; then perform the exercise with the right hand for 25 reps. In all do 4 sets of 25 reps each hand.
2. Application of exercise number one.
   Fig. 76. "L" executes a left arrow punch while "R" blocks with a right push down palm. Fig. 77. "R" changes the right push down palm into a right yang knife hand against "L's" throat.
3. Exercise number two.
   Fig. 78. Begin in basic position. Execute a left push down palm and a right yang knife hand. Fig. 79. The left becomes a yang knife hand while the right becomes a push down palm. Alternate for 25 reps each hand. In all do 4 sets of 25 reps each.
4. Application for exercise number two.
   Fig. 80. "L" delivers a left arrow which "R" blocks with a right push down palm while striking a left yang knife hand to the throat of "L".

74

75

76

77

5. Sparring sets.
   These sparring sets involve the push down palm and the dart fingers thrust (bil jee sao). The latter can be a block (a thrusting block) or a block and strike at the same time. If you are close enough to your opponent or move in toward him, you can reach his eyes. Then the dart fingers thrust becomes a block and strike.

40

78

79

80

Sparring set number one.
Fig. 81. "L" delivers a left
arrow which "R" blocks
with a left push down
palm. Fig. 82. "L" then
delivers a right arrow
which "R" blocks with a
left dart fingers thrust. Do
2 sets of 25 reps.

Sparring set number two.
Fig. 83. "L" executes a
right arrow which "R"
blocks with a right push
down palm. Fig. 84. "L"
then executes a left arrow
which "R" blocks with a
right dart fingers thrust.
Do 2 sets of 25 reps.

81

82

83

84

41

85

86

T'uo Sao

In level one the downward sweep and chop movement was introduced (*Sil Lim Tao*, p.77). The diagonal sweep and chop came into focus in level two (*Chum Kil*, p.56). These moves in Chinese are called *t'uo sao*, which means "escaping hand." In other words, you escape from an opponent's grasp by sweeping downward (or on a diagonal) and chopping the opponent's hand away.

1. Fig. 85. From basic position move left arm down and slant it across the body as shown; keep the wrist straight. Bring the right hand across the chest, palm facing up as shown; keep wrist straight. Fig. 86. Slide the right hand down while bringing the left up. As you near the end of the downward sweep with the right hand the palm should turn towards your body so that you end with a chopping motion. When the movement is completed the hands are in reverse position. Now slide the left hand down while bringing the right up again as in figure 85. Fig. 87. Do another right downward sweep and chop, and then execute a left yang knife hand. Repeat the sequence for 20 reps. Then reverse the sequence for 20 more reps. In other words, start with a left t'uo sao, then a right and another left, followed by a right yang knife hand.

87

42

2. Application.
   Fig. 88. "L" grabs "R's" left arm. "R" counters with a right t'uo sao. Fig. 89. The right downward sweep and chop by "R" is followed immediately by a left yang knife hand to the throat of "L".

88

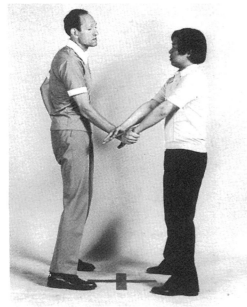

89

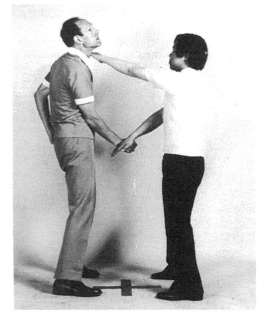

Wing Hand and Yang Knife Hand

1. Exercise.
   Fig. 90. Begin in the basic I.R.A.S. position. Then turn 30° to the right of center while executing a left wing and a right protective hand. Fig. 91. Do a lap sao, i.e., execute a left yang knife hand. Fig. 92. Turn 30° to the left of centre while executing a right wing and left protective hand. Fig. 93. Do a lap sao, i.e., push down with the left protective hand, and execute a right yang knife hand.

90

91

92

93

2. Sparring set.
Fig. 94. Both begin in the basic position. "L" delivers a right arrow punch while turning 30° to the left of center. "R" blocks with a left wing and right protective hand while turning 30° to the right of center. Fig. 95. "R" does a lap sao, i.e., pushes right down and executes a left yang knife hand. "L" blocks with a right wing and a left protective hand. Repeat the sequence for 2 sets of 20 reps. Then shift to the other hand. In other words, "L" begins by delivering a left arrow punch. Repeat for 2 more sets of 20 reps.

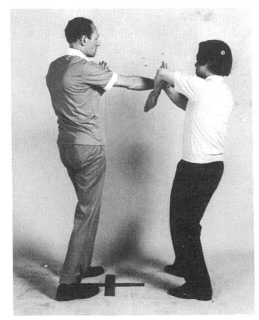

94

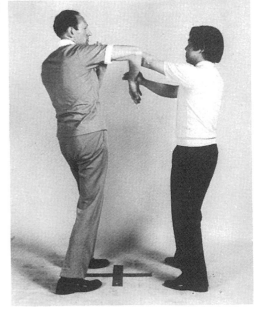

95

Yin Knife Hand and Prayer Palm

1. Exercise.
    Fig. 96. Assume basic position. Turn 30° to the right of center while executing a left wing hand and a right protective hand. Fig. 97. Execute a right prayer palm and a left yin knife hand while turning back to center. Move the right protective hand in front of the left wing hand and change it to a prayer palm pushing it to the side while you change the left wing hand into a yin knife hand. Fig. 98. Turn 30° to the left of center while executing a right wing hand and a left protective hand. Fig. 99. Execute a left prayer palm and a right yin knife hand while turning back to center. Do 3 sets of 50 reps each side.

96

97

98

99

2. Sparring sets.
Sparring set number one: right yin knife hand.
Fig. 100. Assume basic lap sao position, but turn 30° ("L" to the left. "R" to the right). "R" has a left wing hand and a right protective hand, while "L" is ready to strike a right arrow, with the left in lap sao position on "R's" left wrist. Fig. 101. "R" does a right prayer palm and a left yin knife hand while turning 30° to the left of center. "L" blocks with a left wing hand and a right protective hand while turning 30° to the right of center. Return to the position shown in figure 100. Repeat for 2 sets of 50 reps.

100

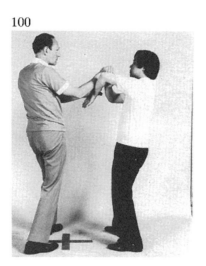

101

Sparring set number two: left yin knife hand.
Fig. 102. Assume basic lap sao position, but turn 30° ("L" to the right, "R" to the left). "R" has a right wing hand and a left protective hand, while "L" is ready to strike a left arrow, with the right in lap sao position on "R's" right wrist. Fig. 103. "R" does a left prayer palm and a right yin knife hand while turning 30° to the right of center. "L" blocks with a right wing hand and a left protective hand while turning 30° to the left of center. Return to position shown in figure 102. Repeat for 2 sets of 50 reps.

102

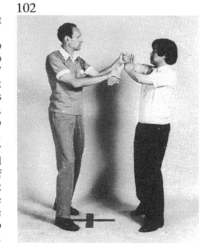

103

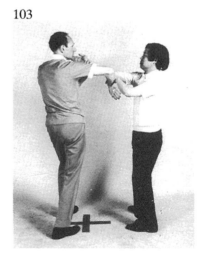

3. Application

Fig. 104. "R" delivers a right arrow. "L" counters with a Wing Chun grab and pull technique. This was introduced in the book of Level Two, Chum Kil, pages 86 to 88 and is called 'pulling hand'. Fig. 105. "R" changes right arrow into a right wing hand. Fig. 106. "R" executes a left prayer palm (pak sao) and a right yin knife hand to "L's" neck.

104

105

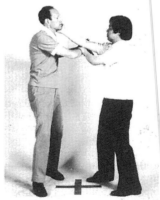

106

Monkey Hand Block (Fook Sao)

1. Exercise.

   Fig. 107. From the basic I.R.A.S. move the left into a monkey hand position. The right remains in the fist back position. Fig. 108. Turn 30° to the left while executing a circular wrist movement. Fig. 109. Return to center with hand in prayer palm position. Change the left to the monkey hand position shown in figure 107. Repeat for 2 sets of 50 reps. Then do the movement with the right hand for 2 sets of 50 reps.

107

108

109

2. Sparring sets.

Fig. 110. Begin in the basic position. "L" throws a right arrow while turning 30° to the left. "R" blocks with a right monkey hand (crossed monkey hand) and at the same time strikes with a left yin knife hand to the neck of "L" while turning 30° to the right. Fig. 111. "L" throws a left arrow while turning 30° to the right of center. "R" blocks with a left monkey hand (crossed monkey hand) and at the same time strikes with a right yin knife hand to the neck of "L" while turning 30° to the left of center. Do 2 sets of 50 reps with each hand.

110

111

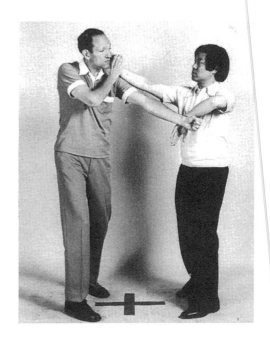

50

Dart Fingers (Bil Jee Sao)

1. Exercise.

Fig. 112. Assume basic I.R.A.S. Execute a left dart fingers thrust. The right hand remains in the fist back position. Fig. 113. Bring the right under the extended left arm as shown. Note that the left bil jee sao is completed, and the right hand is under the elbow of the left arm. Fig. 114. Execute a right dart fingers thrust and retract the left hand to a position under the elbow of the right arm as shown. Then do a left bil jee sao and retract the right, etc. In all do 2 sets of 50 reps with each hand.

112

113

114

2. Applications.
Application number one.

Fig. 115. "L" blocks "R's" right dart fingers thrust with a left prayer palm. Fig. 116. "R" has checked "L's" left prayer palm with a left dart fingers block while at the same time attacking the eyes of "L" with a right dart fingers thrust again. Note that "R" had to move his left hand under his extended right arm shown in figure 115 in order to execute the left dart fingers block.

115   116

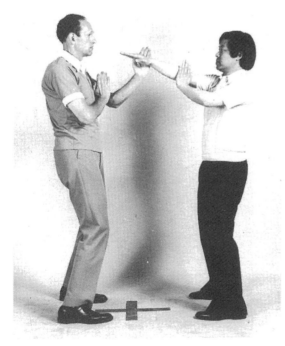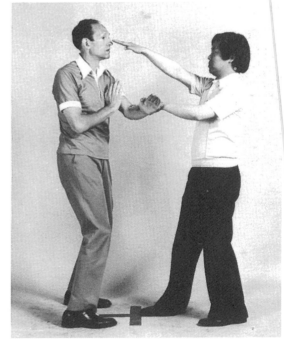

Application number two.
Fig. 117. "R" is in the on guard position and "L" grabs the arms of "R". Fig. 118. "R" changes left protective hand to a left dart fingers block which moves the arms of "L" aside causing "L" to release his hold. At the same time, "R" attacks with a right dart fingers to eyes of "L". Fig. 119. "L" raises both hands to block "R's" right dart fingers attack. Fig. 120. "R" changes right bil jee sao into a push down palm, delivers a left yin knife hand, and steps forward all at the same time.

117

118

119

120

Application number three.
Fig. 121. "L" delivers a left arrow while "R" counters with a right thrusting block, a variation of the dart fingers thrust. Fig. 122. "L" takes a step to the side. Fig. 123. "R" follows "L" and delivers a right yin knife to neck of "L".

122

121

123

54

Cultivating Hand and Yin Knife Hand

The yin knife hand in this movement is like a drop elbow block (*Chum Kil*, p. 52, fig. 154) and the combination itself is called by some the high and low gahng sao and/or the scissors gahng sao.

1. **Exercise.**
    Fig. 124. Begin in basic I.R.A.S. Turn 30° to the right of center while executing a right cultivating hand and a left yin knife hand. Fig. 125. Turn 30° to the left of center while changing the left yin knife hand into a left cultivating hand and the right gahng sao into a right yin knife hand. Do 3 sets of 50 reps each side.

2. **Sparring set.**
    Fig. 126. Begin in the basic position. "L" delivers a left yin knife hand and a right cultivating hand while turning 30° to the right of center. "R" also does a left yin knife hand and a right cultivating hand while turning 30° to the right of center. Fig. 127. "L" delivers a right yin knife hand and a left cultivating hand while turning 30° to the left of center. "R" also does a right yin knife hand and a left cultivating hand while turning 30° to the left of center. Do 4 sets of 25 reps each side.

125

126

124

127

3. Applications.
Application number one.

Fig. 128. "L" begins a left arrow punch. "R" is in an on guard position. Fig. 129. "R" blocks left arrow of "L" with a right cultivating hand, executes a left yin knife hand to "L's" neck, and turns 30° to the right all at the same time. Fig. 130. "L" attempts to counter with a right dart fingers block. Fig. 131. But "R" turns 30° more to the right while retaining the yin knife hand thus effectively countering "L's" right dart fingers block. Fig 132. "R" immediately moves forward with a right semicircular step while changing the left to a prayer palm and the right to a sideward palm strike to the ribs of "L".

128

129

130

131

132

Application number two.
Fig. 133. "L" begins a left arrow punch. "R" is in an on guard position. Fig. 134. "R" blocks left arrow with a left cultivating hand, executes a right yin knife hand to "L's" neck, and turns 30° to the left all at the same time.

133

134

Lai Sao

In level two the Wing Chun grab and pull technique was introduced in conjunction with kicking (*Chum Kil*, pp. 86-88). In Chinese this is called *lai sao*, "pulling hand." The degree of the turn used with the lai sao depends on the position of your opponent and on the fighting conditions. A few degrees may be all that is necessary.

1. **Exercise.**

   Fig. 135. Begin in basic fist back position. Extend both arms in front, parallel with the floor as shown. The right hand is closed as if grasping the wrist of an opponent, and the left hand is open as if ready to push on the elbow of an opponent. Fig. 136. Turn 90° to the right of center. Fig. 137. Turn back to I.R.A.S. The left arm returns to the basic fist back position, while the right arm delivers a sweeping punch. Note that the sweeping punch is delivered while you turn. *The sweeping punch* (or puppet punch) can be combined with the lai sao. It is always executed with a turn so that the full momentum of your body will be behind the punch. Fig. 138. The foreknuckles provide the point of contact rather than the knuckles. Fig. 139. In addition, there is a turn of the wrist as the punch is delivered. Fig. 140. The right sweeping punch changes to a right downward palm strike. Then return the right arm to the basic fist back position. Although the downward palm strike in combat is directed to the tan tien area, in training the arm is thrust straight forward so that the arm is parallel with the floor (*Sil Lim Tao*, pp. 54-56). Repeat this exercise for 3 sets of 10 reps. Then do it for the other side for an equal number of sets and reps. In other words, extend both arms, but the left hand should be closed and the right hand open. Turn 90° to the left of centre. Turn back to centre while bringing right arm to fist back position while delivering a left sweeping punch. Then do a left downward palm strike, and return left arm to fist back position.

135

138

136   137

139   140

59

2. Applications.

Application number one.

Fig. 141. "R" attempts a right arrow punch, but "L" counters with a lai sao while turning about 90° to the right. Fig. 142. "L" then executes a right sweeping punch to the ribs of "R" while turning back to center. Fig. 143. "R" blocks with a right jeet sao. Fig. 144. "L" counters by moving forward and using his shoulder. The use of the shoulder in combination with the push down palm was discussed in volume two (Chum Kil, pp. 60-61).

141

142

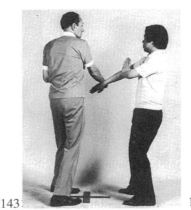

143

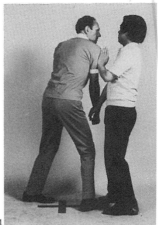

144

Application number two.
Fig. 145. As a counter to "L's" lai sao as shown in figure 141, "R" executes a right B.D.E.P. while moving forward. This must be done before your opponent begins a sweeping punch.

Application number three.
Fig. 146. As a counter to "L's" lai sai shown in figure 141, "R" executes a left dart fingers block, causing "L" to release the lai sao. When "R's" right arm is free, he strikes with a yang knife hand to "L's" throat. Note that "R" had to move under his own trapped right arm to deliver the initial right dart fingers block.

Application number four.
Fig. 147. "L" delivers a left arrow punch which "R" blocks with a left wing hand (crossed wing hand). Fig. 148. "R" then follows up with a lai sao and a kick. Note that it is not necessary for "R" to turn in executing the lai sao and kick. "R" simply pulls "L" forward and kicks. "R" also could have kicked "L" in the groin.

145

146

147

148

Exercises to Strengthen the Torso and Legs for Kicking.

Physiologists tell us that in order to maintain bodily efficiency moderate exercise in which the heart is noticeably increased should be engaged in for 20 minutes at least 3 times a week. Wing Chun movements and supplementary exercises will have a very beneficial effect on the cardio-vascular system.

1. **Sit ups with hands clasped behind head.**
    Figs. 149, 150 and 151. Lie flat on the floor with your feet under a heavy object if necessary, with your hands clasped behind your head. Sit up pulling your head forward with your arms as you do so, and try to touch your knees with your elbows. Breathe out completely as you sit up and bend forward. Inhale slowly and deeply as you return to the starting position. Do not strain, but bring your head and elbows as close to your knees as possible. As you sit up your feet will be inclined to rise and spoil the movement. To avoid this, place your feet under the foot of a bed, or under the edge of a bureau. This exercise catches the first two ridges of your abdominal muscles mostly, thus bringing a more direct massage upon your stomach and building a heavier muscular coating over your solar plexus, or thoracic arch. The important part to observe when performing this exercise is to keep your back round. Don't keep your back straight when raising or lowering. Do 3 sets of 2 minutes each.

2. **Twist with hands clasped behind head.**
    Figs. 152, 153. Assume a sitting position, chest high, neck firm, elbows well back, chin up, legs spread. Twist the trunk to the left as far as possible, keeping the head up, chest high, elbows back, and legs flat.

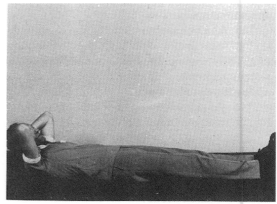

149

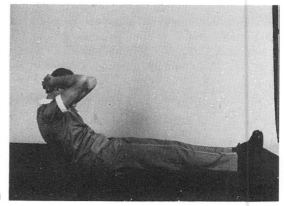

150

151

152

Return to starting position and repeat to the right. Continue in this alternate fashion. This exercise will strengthen the lateral muscles of the trunk and the long back muscles. Do 3 sets of 2 minutes each.

3. Twist with arms extended.

Figs. 154, 155. If you are short-winded this fine abdominal exercise will correct it. Although your whole upper body is affected, the severest action is upon your entire abdominal and lumbar region. Sit on the floor with your feet spread widely apart. Hold your arms out level with your shoulders. Now, twist around from your waist as far as possible to the left. Do not change the position of your arms. Let them follow the trunk. Return to the starting position, and twist to the right. Continue in this alternate fashion. Remember to revolve from your waist with your arms always at the same angle. Do 3 sets of 2 minutes each.

153

155

154

4. Alternate leg thrust.

Figs. 156, 157. Lie flat on your back with your hands on the floor by your hips and your legs stretched our straight. Slowly draw up the knee of one leg as close to your body as possible. Thrust your leg straight out from this position, without allowing the heel to touch the floor. Repeat the exercise with your other leg; alternate legs. Do 3 sets of 2 minutes each.

5. Alternate leg raise.

Figs. 158, 159. Assume the same position as for the previous exercise. Slowly raise one leg toward your head. Lower your leg to the floor, then repeat with your other leg. Raise your leg as far towards your head as you can. This exercise and the previous one are excellent for lower abdomen and pelvis muscles. Do 3 sets of 2 minutes each.

6. Side kick exercise.

Figs. 160, 161. Recline on your right side as shown. Fig. 160. Bend left leg. Fig. 161. Execute a kick as wide as possible. Snap the leg. After completing 3 sets for 2 minutes, shift to the left side and do kicks with the right leg for an equal amount of time.

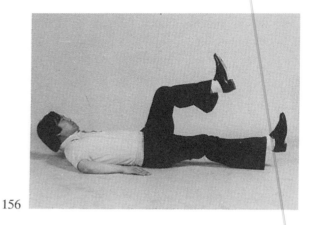

156

158

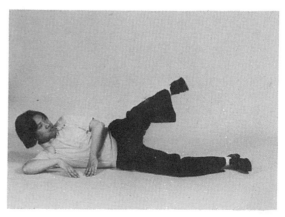

160

157

159

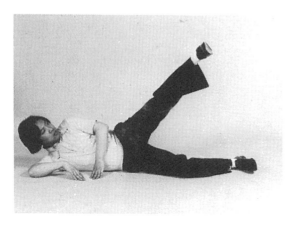

161

65

162 163 164

7. **Knee twist.**
   Fig. 162. Stand with your arms by your sides, legs straight, and feet together. Fig. 163. Bend your knees and raise your arms into a fist back position. Fig. 164. Twist knees to the left. Fig. 165. Twist knees to the right. Do 3 sets of 2 minutes each.

8. **Quarter squat with leg extension.**
   Fig. 166. Assume basic fist back position but with feet at a 45° angle. Do a quarter squat. Fig. 167. Extend the left leg as shown. Return to the quarter squat position. Fig. 168. Then extend the right leg as shown. Continue alternately for 3 sets of 2 minutes each.

167

165

166

168

9. Relaxing and stretching movement.

The Chinese character for "big" is used to describe this exercise. Fig. 169. Stand with your feet shoulder width apart and your arms out level with your shoulders. Fig. 170a. Turn 90° to the left as shown and raise the right leg. Fig. 170b. Bend forward as shown and extend the right leg as far back as possible. Return to position as in figure 169. Fig. 171. Turn 90° to the right, raise the left leg, bend forward as shown and extend the left leg as far back as possible. Return to position as in figure 169. Repeat alternately for 3 sets of 3 minutes each.

170a

170b

169

171

68

10. Side bend exercise.

Fig. 172. Begin in the position shown in figure 169. Bend to the right and touch the floor with the fingers of your right hand while extending your left leg as far as possible. Return to original position. Then bend to the left, etc. Repeat alternately for 3 sets of 2 minutes each.

11. Leg stretch in bow and arrow stance. Exercise number one.

Fig. 173. Assume a deep and wide horse-riding stance with feet pointed straight forward and fists back. Fig. 174. Turn to the right and bend the right leg, but the knee should not go beyond the right foot. Keep the left leg straight in a straight line with the head. This stance is used in a number of Kung Fu systems. Wing Chun uses it only for puroses of exercise and not for combat. Turn back to the original position. Then turn to the left and repeat. Do alternately for 3 sets of 2 minutes each.

172

173   174

69

Exercise number two.

Begin in a deep horse stance shown in figure 173. Fig. 175. Turn to the right and bend the right leg as far as possible, i.e. beyond the right foot. Keep the left leg as straight as possible. Turn back to original position. Then turn to the left and repeat. Do alternately for 3 sets of 2 minutes each.

175

12. **Squat on one leg.**

Sit on a low stool. Extend the right leg. Put hands in an on guard position. The inquisitive hand should be opposite from the extended leg, e.g., when the right leg is extended, then the left hand should be inquisitive. From the sitting position, raise yourself up with the strength of your left leg while keeping your hands in the on guard position. Lower yourself to the stool and repeat. Repeat for 2 minutes. Then extend the left leg and continue for another 2 minutes. In all repeat the exercise for 2 sets of 2 minutes each leg.

Kicking Exercises

1. **Front kick from I.R.A.S.**

Fig. 176. Assume I.R.A.S. with right hand in the inquisitive position and the left as protective. Fig. 177. Do a right front kick and return to I.R.A.S. Fig. 178. then do a left front kick while changing the positions of the hands. The left is changed to inquistitive and the right to protective. Do 2 sets of 20 reps with each leg.

176   178

2. **Front kick and thrusting block from I.R.A.S. (not illustrated).**

Assume I.R.A.S. with left hand inquisitive and right protective. Do a right front kick and a left thrusting block. Return to I.R.A.S. Change positions of hands so that the right hand is inquisitive and the left is protective. Then do a left front kick and a right thrusting block. Alternate for 2 sets of 20 reps each leg.

3. Front kick with double snake hand from a charging stance.

Fig. 179. Assume a charging stance with right leg forward and with hands in a double open hand block position. Fig. 180. Deliver a right front kick while executing a double snake hand. Repeat for 2 sets of 20 reps. Then do the same with the left leg for another 2 sets of 20 reps. Figure 181 shows an application of this movement. "L" delivers a double arrow punch which "R" counters with a double snake hand and a right front kick.

180

179

181

4. Front kick moving.
Fig. 182. Place feet together with hands in a fist back position, and do a quarter squat. Fig. 183. Execute a left front kick. Fig. 184. Put the left leg down in front of the right as shown. Fig. 185. Do a right front kick. Then place the right leg in front of the left. Alternate the legs. In a word, when you kick, you take one step forward. After ten steps forward, reverse the procedure and kick while stepping back for ten paces back to the original position. Do two sets.

182

183

184

185

5. Hammer kick.

The name for this kick derives from the movement of the foot which is like a hammer driving a nail into a wall. This is just a training routine for the front kick with the toes pointed outward and for the side kick. It is a difficult exercise to do, but constant practice will help you develop necessary hip strength and flexibility. Be persistent and patient. Fig. 186. Assume the basic I.R.A.S. Fig. 187. Execute a right front kick with the toes out. Fig. 188. Move leg and foot to the left while delivering a second kick with a snap. In level two we noted that the initial front kick is executed by a movement of the hip joint (hip flexion). Once the first kick is completed, bend the knee slightly and then deliver a snapping kick by making a knee extension (*Chum Kil*, p.83). Return to the basic I.R.A.S. and continue for 20 reps. Then do another set. Repeat the exercise with the left leg. *Application*. Fig. 189. "R" executes a right front kick, but "L" moves back to avoid it. Fig. 190. "R" then delivers a right side kick to catch the retreating "L".

186

188

189

187

190

191   192

6. **Alternative exercise.**
   If you find the hammer kick exercise too difficult to begin with, then start with this alternative exercise. Fig. 191. Assume a basic on guard position, left hand inquisitive and right hand protective. Execute a left front kick. Fig. 192. Then deliver a left side kick while pivoting on the right leg. Return to original position. Repeat for 2 sets of 20 reps. Then do the same with the right leg.

7. **Alternate side kick with pivot.**
   Assume basic I.R.A.S. Turn the right foot by pivoting on the heel and sliding on the sole of the foot until the toes point to the right of centre; 30°–45° should be sufficient. While you are turning with the right leg, execute a left side kick. Return the left leg so that the toes are pointing 30°–45° to the left of centre while at the same time executing a right side kick. Continue alternating until you have completed 20 kicks with each leg. Then do another set. This is an excellent movement to practice on the wooden dummy.

8. **Side kicks with a pivot.**
   Begin in basic I.R.A.S. Pivot on the right foot and execute a left side kick as in the preceding exercise. Continue doing left side kicks for 3 minutes. Then return the left leg to the floor so that the toes are pointing 30°–45° to the left of centre while at the same time execute a right side kick. Continue doing right side kicks for three minutes. In all do 3 sets of 3 minutes each side.

9. **Low wing and side kick.**
   Assume basic on guard position with the right hand as inquisitive and the left as protective. Turn 30° to the left, while executing a right low wing and delivering a right side kick. The left hand remains in the protective position. Turn back to basic position and repeat for 10 reps. Then shift the hands so that the left is now inquisitive and the right is protective. Then do a left low wing and a left side kick for another 10 reps. In all do 2 sets of 10 reps each side.

8. Side kick while jumping.

This is an exercise and a type of Wing Chun kick. It is used when your opponent is crowding you so that you have no space to deliver a kick. You jump aside while simultaneously executing a side kick. Figures 193, 194, and 195 illustrate the movement. Practice it for 3 sets of 10 reps each side. In combat be careful not to show any intention before you start the jump and kick. As with punches, you must be relaxed. Practice slowly at first. Speed will come with time.

194

193

195

11. High kicks.

As mentioned in level two, Wing Chun kicks are low. The stomach and ribs of an opponent are as high as you would want to go in an attack (*Chum Kil*, p. 82). In training, however, you can practice high kicks as shown in figures 196 a and b. This type of practice will increase your flexibility and thus make the low kicks easier.

196a   196b

12. Supplementary equipment for training.

Yip Man often had his students make use of a young tree. One end of a rope was tied to the trunk of a young tree while the other end was tied to the ankle of the student. Various kicking movements could then be practised against the tension of the tree. Instead of a tree, you can use a spring or a series of springs suspended from the ceiling to about the height of your chest. Stand on one leg and fasten your other ankle to a belt attached to the springs. Pull downward and work against the tension of the springs. Such a device can help you develop great power in your hips and legs. Sandbags are extremely useful also. Very often they are made of double layers of canvas, with strong metal eyes for wall mounting. These bags can be used to practise punches and kicks alike. The serious student who has mastered level three should seriously consider the purchase of a wooden dummy in order to refine his or her techniques. We intend to cover the wooden dummy movements and their applications in a later volume.

Penetrating Kicks

Before attempting advanced kicking, you must be secure in the basic moves covered in level two. Your supporting leg must be stable, and you must be very good with regular kicks before going on to penetrating kicks, otherwise you will be off balance. In advanced kicking, when the kick lands you use your back and hips, i.e., you use your body to give the kick more power, like the optional wrist movements with arrow punches. The term in Chinese for this extra snap to the kick is called *chün sum gür,* "to go through the heart of," in other words, to penetrate deeply. In the case of a front kick for example, the extra snap would cause the heel to dig into the opponent more deeply. Yip Man said that if the chün sum gür were done properly, that would be the end of the opponent. There is a saying in Wing Chun: "One kick of the chün sum gür and even a good master will be finished". The legs are about four times as strong as the arms, but in all kicking, you must measure the distance to your opponent with your eyes in order to determine how close you have to move before delivering a kick. Do not signal the kick by moving your shoulders. But after you have begun to deliver the kick you can use your body to give it extra power once it lands. This is the secret of chün sum gür.

Final Movements in the Bil Jee Set

The final movements in the Bil Jee Set involve first of all one in which you bend over as in figure 197. This is followed by a guarding movement with the hands and a right front kick as in figure 198. The application and meaning of these moves are illustrated. Fig. 199. "L" is attacking "R" who is bent over, perhaps getting up off the floor. Fig. 200. "R" counters by blocking with his hands and executing a right front kick against "L".

197

198

199

200

Free Attack

The following are some examples of Wing Chun against another style. Fig. 214a. "L" is beginning a right side kick. "R" is in a Wing Chun on guard position. Fig. 214b. "R" pivots on right foot and executes a left side kick to the side of "L's" left knee, i.e., "L's" supporting leg. "R's" turn while kicking is comparable to turning while punching. The turn gives extra power to the kick. Fig. 215a. "R", in a Wing Chun on guard stance, attempts a right front kick. "L", in a non Wing Chun posture, tries to block "R's" kick with his own left leg as shown. Fig. 215b. "R" has moved his right leg back and around by a quick external rotation movement and has executed a kick to the side of "R's" knee. At the same time "R" does a right prayer palm, pushing "L's" left elbow down.

214a

215a

214b

215b

The external rotation block and/or kick was introduced in level two (*Chum Kil,* p.81). A basic Wing Chun principle is that when an opponent's hand or leg goes out, search for his body and not his hand or leg. In this case, rather than using power against "L's" blocking leg, "R" moved around it and attacked "L's" supporting leg. Fig. 216a. "L" is in a karate stance while "R" is in a Wing Chun on guard stance. Fig. 216b. "L" steps forward with his right leg while moving his left elbow up to execute an elbow strike. "R" blocks "L's" elbow with a right prayer palm while moving left leg back. Fig. 216c. "L" has moved left leg up and has pivoted to the right in an effort to complete the left elbow strike to "R". But "R" continues the right prayer palm, which causes "L's" elbow to be diverted. At the same time "R" executes a left yin knife hand to the neck of "L" and brings right foot down forcibly on the back of "L's" left knee with a stamping kick.

216a

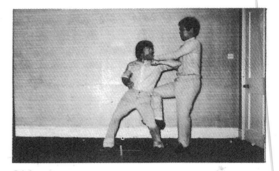

216c

216b

84

Fig. 217a. "L" is in a karate stance while "R" is in a Wing Chun on guard stance. Fig. 217b. "L" begins a round house (360° turn) knife hand attack. "L" reached the position shown in figure 217b. by pivoting on his left leg in a counter clockwise movement. Fig. 217c. "L" continues his pivot and is ready to deliver a strike with his right hand. But "R" has countered with a right front kick to "L's" right hip. Fig. 217d. This is an alternative for "R" if "L" completes his 360° turn. "R" blocks the right arm strike of "L" by executing a left side kick to "L's" right knee while turning. At the same time "L" does a lai sao.

217a

217c

217b

217d

Fig. 218a. "L" is in a karate stance while "R" is in a Wing Chun on guard stance. Fig. 218b. "L" steps forward with his left leg and uses his left hand to push "R's" inquisitive hand down while preparing to punch with his right hand. Fig. 218c. "L" attempts a punch with his right hand which "R" blocks with a left prayer palm while executing a right arrow to "L's" head and a right front kick to the stomach and groin of "L".

218a

218b

218c

Fig. 219a. "L" is in a karate stance while "R" is in I.R.A.S. position with the right hand as inquisitive and the left as protective. Fig. 219b. "L" steps forward with his left leg while attempting to execute a mountain punch. But "R" has moved forward with his right leg while delivering a double arrow punch. The Wing Chun double arrow reaches "L" before he can complete his mountain punch because the Wing Chun double arrow is a straight line punch while the arms are bent like the horns on cattle for the mountain punch.

Remember always the spirit of Shaolin and use your skills only for self defence, to protect the weak, and to enforce justice. Confucius says: "Do not do to others what you would not want others to do to you." The world, however, is a violent place; and "down these mean streets a man must go who is not himself mean, who is neither tarnished nor afraid." Although Lao Tzu asserts that a sage achieves results without violence, it is equally true that "no one can purify another" (*The Dhammapada*). A violent man may force you to contend with him. Then remember "in a heart that is One with Nature, though the body contends, there is no violence."

219a

219b

Summary of Punches

Punches are listed according to level and in the order in which they were first introduced. It has been said, "Each waking moment is like a rung on an endless ladder. We climb, only by rising from those which have come before." In Wing Chun, the Sil Lim Tao is the first rung on the ladder of perfection. The basic principles, punches, and blocks are introduced on this first level and are carried through the next two levels where additional movements are added; and the techniques of the Sil Lim Tao are integrated with those of the sophisticated Chum Kil and Bil Jee. Lap Sao and Dahn Chi Sao are introduced at the end of level one. Luk Sao variations and Lap Sao while turning are practiced in level two. Since these exercises are an essential part of Wing Chun, you should include them in your training schedule as part of your sparring.

Level One
1. Double elbow punch.
2. Arrow punch.
3. Vertical palm strike.
4. Push down palm (also block).
5. Extended hands (fac sao).
6. Yang knife hand.
7. Dart fingers thrust (bil jee sao), also a block.
8. Cannon punch.
9. Sideward palm strike.
10. Downward palm strike.
11. Yin knife hand (also a block).
12. Downward sweep and chop (t'uo sao), escaping hand.

Level Two
1. Shortened punches.
2. Wrist movements with arrow punches.
3. Eye of the phoenix.
4. Double arrow punch.
5. Parallel elbow punch.
6. Corkscrew punch (similar to an uppercut in boxing).
7. Diagonal sweep and chop.
8. Double snake hand combined with double vertical palm strike.
9. In addition to the new movements, the blocks, punches, and strikes of the Sil Lim Tao are combined with the turns, footwork, and kicks of level two.

Level Three
1. Bowing down elbow punch (also a block).
2. Jeet sao (obstructing hand), also a block.
3. Sweeping punch; may be combined with lai sao.
4. In addition, there are complex combinations in which elbows, palms, and fingers are combined with rapid leg movements as one defends and attacks at the same time.

Note: On levels two and three, punches and blocks often are combined with turns and other footwork. On all levels attack is accentuated, and it is an attack in which there is no set pattern. On all levels, too, one blocks and hits simultaneously.

Summary of Blocks

The blocks are listed also according to level and in the order in which they were first introduced. In addition, they are grouped according to the areas which they defend primarily (high, middle, and low). In some cases several areas are included. Review the centreline theory described in level one (*Sil Lim Tao*, pp. 9-10). The extended hand in the fighting stance is known as the "inquisitive hand" (man sao) while the hand behind is called the "protective hand" (wu sao) acting as a rear guard.

High (From head to solar plexus)

Level One
1. Open hand block (tan sao); also called palm-up block, palm-up hand, and beggar hand.
2. Monkey hand (fook sao); also called elbow in bent block and bridge-on-hand.
3. Circular wrist (hieung sao).
4. Prayer palm (pak sao).
5. Snake hand (jut sao); also called shock hand, jerking hand, and retracting hand.
6. Thrusting block (knife hand and dart fingers).
7. Wing hand (bong sao).

Level Two
1. Ting sao (thrusting forward hand).
2. Lan sao (intercepting hand).
3. Double snake hand (with double vertical palm strike).
4. Cheh sao (breaking hand) and tying a knot.
5. T'oh sao (to bear upon the palm).
6. Lai sao (pulling hand) with kicks.

Level Three
1. Bowing down elbow punch.
2. Bowing down elbow punch and dart fingers thrusting block.
3. Jeet sao.

Middle (From solar plexus to groin)
Level One
1. Drop elbow or knife hand block (jum sao).
2. Push down palm.
3. Sliding hand.
4. Cultivating hand (gahng sao).
5. Low wing hand.

Level Two
1. Lai sao with kicks.
2. Yin knife hand and cultivating hand while turning (introduced but not discussed until level three).

Level Three
1. Yin knife hand and cultivating hand while turning.
2. Lai sao with sweeping punch.

Low (groin to feet)
Level One
1. Cultivating hand.

Level Two
1. General principle: block a kick with a kick.
2. Low wing.
3. Push down palm while turning.
4. External rotation block.
5. Side kick as a block.

Level Three
1. Yin knife hand and cultivating hand while turning.
2. Penetrating kicks (chün sum gür).

89

Summary of Stances, Steps and Kicks

Level One
1.   Front stance or Internal Rotated Adduction Stance (I.R.A.S.).

Level Two
1.   Side stance or sitting horse stance.
2.   Charging stance.
3.   Sliding step (a powerful movement when combined with a bong sao).
4.   Triangular step.
5.   External rotation kick (and block).
6.   Front kicks (toes up, toes out).
7.   Front kick from a turn.
8.   Side kicks (to ribs, knee, and ankle).
9.   T'o kick combination (trip and kick).

Level Three
1.   Semicircular sliding step.
2.   Side kick while jumping aside.
3.   Penetrating kicks (chün sum gür).
4.   Right front kick after being bent over (final movements of Bil Jee Set).
5.   Side kick variations.
6.   Stamping kick.

A COMPLETE WING CHUN TRAINING PROGRAMME

Introductory Remarks

The Sil Lim Tao Set is a model for correct movements; therefore do not neglect it. The wing hand, open hand block, monkey hand, circular wrist, and prayer palm are of most important *defensive* moves of the Sil Lim Tao. On the same level, the arrow punch, vertical palm, and extended hands (as a preparation for the yang knife hand) are the most important *offensive* moves. Always practice the open hand block, circular wrist, monkey hand, and prayer palms very slowly. Incorporate the single-leg stance into your training (*Chum Kil,* p.80). Raise your left leg while practising the kowtow sequence of the Sil Lim Tao Set, i.e., monkey hand, open hand block, circular wrist, and prayer palm, with the left hand. Raise your right leg while practising with the right hand.

Exercises for Second Day and Third Day of Training.

Do three sets of 20 reps. for each side on the exercises.

1. *Arrow punch while turning.*
   From the basic position turn 30° to the right while striking a left arrow. Then do the same to the left. Repeat alternatively.

2. *Arrow punch stepping forward and back.*
   From the basic position deliver a left arrow punch while taking a left triangular step. Execute a right arrow punch while returning to the basic position. Then strike a left arrow punch from the horse stance. Deliver another left arrow punch while sliding the left foot forward again. Continue this sequence for the required number of reps. Then repeat the sequence with the right leg and arm.

3. *Wing hand and protective hand while turning.*
   From the basic position turn right 45° while executing a left wing hand and bringing the right one into a protective hand position. Then turn left 45° while changing the right protective hand into a bong sao and moving the left into a protective hand position. Perform this alternatively.

4. *Lap sao or warding off hands sparring set (Sil Lim Tao, p.74).*

5. *Yin knife hand and prayer palm.*
   See figures 96-99 of this volume.

6. *Open hand block (tan sao) and arrow punch while turning.*
   From basic position turn 30° to the right while executing a right open hand block and a left arrow punch. Then turn 30° to the left while doing a left open hand block and a right arrow punch.

7. *Cultivating hand (gahng sao) and arrow punch while turning.*
From basic position turn 30° to the right while executing a right cultivating hand and a left arrow punch. Then turn 30° to the left while doing a left cultivating hand and a right arrow punch.

8. *Yin knife hand exercise while turning.*
See figures 39-41 of this volume.

9. *Triangular step with push down palm and arrow punch.*
Take a left triangular step while executing a left arrow punch and a right push down palm. Then do a right triangular step while executing a right arrow punch and a left push down palm. Continue the moves alternately for the required number of reps. and sets.

10. *Double arrow punch while turning.*
From the basic position turn 30° to the right while executing a double arrow punch. The left hand is above the right. Then turn 30° to the left while doing another double arrow punch. The right hand is above the left. Continue the moves alternately.

11. *Thrusting block and yin knife hand.*
Assume an I.R.A.S. on guard position with the left as inquisitive and the right as protective. Execute a thrusting block with the left. Then turn 30° to the right of centre while delivering a yin knife hand with the left. Then do the movement with the right hand. Continue the moves alternately.

12. *Bong Sao, jut sao, and yang knife hand.*
From the basic I.R.A.S. turn 30° to the left of centre while executing a right wing hand with the left held as protective. Then change the right bong sao to a jut sao and the protective hand to a left yang knife hand while turning 30° to the right of centre. Convert the yang knife hand into a left snake hand and the right jut sao to a right yang knife hand while turning 30° to the left of centre. Return to I.R.A.S. and then turn 30° to the right of centre while executing a left wing hand with the right held as protective. Change the left bong sao to a jut sao and the protective hand to a right yang knife hand while turning 30° to the left of centre. Convert the yang knife hand into a right snake hand and the left jut sao to a left yang knife hand while turning 30° to the right of centre. Return to I.R.A.S. Repeat the original cycle beginning with the right bong sao. Alternate for the required number of reps. and sets.

13. *Triangular step with cultivating hand and arrow punch.*
Take a left triangular step while executing a left arrow punch and a right cultivating hand. Then do a right triangular step while executing a right arrow punch and a left cultivating hand. Continue the movements alternately.

14. *Triangular step with arrow punch.*
    Slide forward with the left leg while executing a left arrow punch. Then slide forward with the right leg while delivering a right arrow. The left is retracted to the centreline near the chest. Practice this forward motion for the specified number of reps.; then do the triangular step and arrow punch while going backwards for an equal number of reps. As in the case of all the exercises, do 3 sets.

15. *Triangular step with wing hand.*
    Execute a left triangular step and left wing hand with right hand in a protective position. Then do a right triangular step and a right wing hand. Continue moves alternately.

16. *Sliding step with wing hand.*
    Practice the sliding step with left wing hand and the left leg leading. The right hand is held in the protective position. After the required number of reps, practice the sliding step with the right wing hand and the right leg leading. As in the case of all the exercises, do 3 sets. This is a very powerful and exceedingly important movement. Remember that the wing hand moves with the entire body. Yip Man used the wing hand combined with the push down palm very effectively. He would execute a lap sao with the protective hand to chop aside the opponent's arm and change the wing hand to a push down palm to the tan tien area.

17. *Ting sao and parallel elbow punch while turning.*
    From basic position perform a double ting sao. Then turn 90° to the right while sweeping the left elbow as if to strike an opponent on your right. At the same time move the right arm above the left. The forearms should be parallel at the completion of the movement. Return to double ting sao position. Turn 90° to the left while sweeping the right elbow and moving the left arm above the right. Continue moves alternately.

18. *Lan sao and front kick.*
    From basic position turn 90° to the left while executing a left lan sao. The right arm remains in fist back position. Follow this with a left front kick. Return leg to floor. Then turn 90° to the right of centre and perform a right lan sao while returning left arm to basic position. Follow with a right front kick. Return leg to floor. Continue alternately.

19. *Low wing while turning.*
    From basic position turn 30° to the right while executing a left low wing hand and a right protective hand. Then turn 30° to the left of centre and do a right low wing hand while raising the left hand into a protective position. Repeat alternately.

20. *Cheh sao exercise.*
From basic position turn 90° to the left. Do the cheh sao exercise alternately until you have completed the required number of reps. Then assume basic position. Turn 90° to the right and repeat the exercise alternately. In all do 3 sets on each side.

21. *Extended hand and drop elbow block.*
From basic position perform a left fac sao. From extended hand position, execute a drop elbow block. Return to extended hand position and repeat for a required number of reps. Then practice the exercise with the right arm.

22. *Extended hand and push down palm.*
From basic position perform left fac sao. From extended hand position, execute a push down palm. Return to extended hand position and repeat for required number of reps. Then practice the exercise with the right arm.

23. *Push down palm and cannon punch while turning.*
From basic position turn 30° to the right while doing a push down palm with the left hand. The right hand remains in place. Then deliver a left cannon punch while turning back to the basic horse stance position. After you return the left hand to the basic fist back position, turn 30° to the left and repeat the cycle with the right hand. Continue alternately.

24. *Triangular step with vertical palm strike.*
Execute a left triangular step and a left vertical palm strike with right hand in a protective position. Then do a right triangular step and a right vertical palm strike with the left hand in a protective position. Continue the moves alternately.

25. *Sideward palm strike to the ribs while turning.*
From the basic position turn 30° to the right while executing a left sideward palm strike to the ribs. Then turn 30° to the left of centre while executing a right sideward palm strike to the ribs. Continue the moves alternately. Note that the hand not executing the sideward palm strike is held in a protective position.

26. *Yin knife hand while turning.*
From the basic position turn 30° to the right while executing a left yin knife hand to the neck. Remember as in the case of the sideward palm strike to the ribs that the striking surface is the edge of the hand. Then turn 30° to the left of centre while executing a right yin knife hand. Retract left hand to protective position as the right hand executes the yin knife hand. Return the right hand to the protective position as the left executes the yin knife hand. Continue to strike alternately.

27. *Cultivating hand, yin knife hand, and butterfly palms.*
This exercise is based on a wooden dummy movement. For the proper execution of the cultivating hand and yin knife hand combination (called by some the high and low gahng sao) see figures 124 and 125. Turn 30° to the right while executing a right gahng sao and a left yin knife hand. Remember that in this movement, the yin knife hand is like a drop elbow block. Then both hands change to butterfly palms while turning back to the centre. In this case the left hand delivers a vertical palm strike, while the right delivers a downward palm strike. Turn 30° to the left while executing a left gahng sao and a right yin knife hand. Then deliver the butterfly palms while turning back to basic position. Now the right hand is above and the left below. Double palm strikes are called "butterfly palms." Continue the movements alternately.

28. *Double sideward palm strike to ribs and double yin knife hand to neck.*
Assume basic I.R.A.S. Move arms to a double open hand block. Then complete a circular wrist movement with each hand followed by a double sideward palm strike to the ribs (butterfly palms). Return to a double open hand block followed by a double yin knife hand to the neck. Return to a double tan sao and repeat the cycle for the required number of reps. and sets. This exercise is based on a wooden dummy sequence.

29. *Open hand block and sideward palm strike.*
Assume a fighting stance in the I.R.A.S. with the right hand as inquisitive and the left as protective. Then take a right semicircular step while changing the right hand to an open hand block and the left hand to a sideward palm strike to the ribs. Return to basic position with the left hand as inquisitive and the right as protective. Then take a left semicircular step. The left hand changes to an open hand block and the right hand to a sideward palm strike. Alternate for the required number of reps. and sets.

30. *B.D.E.P. with protective hand while turning 30°.*
From basic position execute a left B.D.E.P. and a right protective hand while turning 30° to the right of centre. Then deliver a right B.D.E.P. and a left protective hand while turning 30° to the left of centre. Continue alternately.

31. *Triangular step with B.D.E.P.*
Execute a left triangular step and a left B.D.E.P. with right hand in a protective position. Then do a right triangular step and a right B.D.E.P. with left hand in a protective position. Continue the moves alternately.

32. *Corkscrew punch exercise.*
From basic position turn 30° to the left while executing a right wing hand and bringing the left hand into a protective position. The wing hand changes into a corkscrew punch while turning until you reach 90° to the left. The left hand remains in a protective position. Return to position in which you are 30° to the left with your right in the wing hand position. Repeat the exercise for the required number of reps. and sets. Then complete an equal number of reps. and sets to the opposite side.

33. *Drop elbow block and yang knife hand to throat.*
From basic position execute a drop elbow block with left arm. Follow this immediately with a left yang knife hand. Do it in one fluid movement. Keep the elbow relaxed. Return to drop elbow position and repeat for required number of reps. Do the same for the right arm. In all do three sets each arm.

34. *Exercise for downward palm strike to tan tien.*
From basic position execute an open hand block with left hand. Thrust arm forward along centreline while moving fingers downward. In training the arm is thrust straight forward so that the arm is parallel with floor. The heel of the palm is up, and the main force of the strike is centred in the heel of the palm. Return to open hand block position and repeat for required number of reps. before assuming the basic position. Then switch to the right arm for an equal number of reps. Continue until you have completed 3 sets with each arm.

35. *T'uo sao with arrow punch.*
From basic position execute a right t'uo sao followed by a left arrow punch. The reverse the sequence, i.e., do a left t'uo sao followed by a right arrow punch. Continue the movements alternately.

36. *T'uo sao with yang knife hand.*
From basic position execute a right t'uo sao followed by a left yang knife hand. Reverse the sequence by doing a left t'uo sao and a right yang knife hand. Continue alternately.

37. *T'uo sao with yin knife hand.*
From basic position execute a right t'uo sao followed by a left yin knife hand. Reverse the sequence with a left t'uo sao and a right yin knife hand.

38. *Push down palm and yang knife hand.*
Begin in basic position. Do a left push down palm. The left push down palm changes to a left yang knife hand. Repeat for the required number of times. Then perform the exercise with the right hand for an equal number of reps. In all do 3 sets with each hand.

39. *Alternate push down palm and yang knife hand.*
From basic position execute a left push down palm and a right yang knife hand. Then do a right push down palm and a left yang knife hand. Continue alternately.

40. *Snake hand and dart fingers.*
From the basic position, move your left hand into a snake hand position (jut sao). Then execute a left dart fingers attack (bil jee sao). Return to the snake hand position. Repeat for the required number of reps. Then do the same with the right hand an equal number of times. In all do 3 sets with each hand.

41. *Alternate dart fingers thrust.*
Assume basic I.R.A.S. Execute a left bil jee sao. The right hand remains in fist back position. Then bring the right under the extended left arm. Execute a right dart fingers thrust and retract the left hand to a position under the elbow of the right arm. See figures 113 and 114. Continue alternately for required number of reps. and sets.

42. *B.D.E.P. and yin knife hand.*
From the basic position execute a left B.D.E.P. while turning 30° to right of centre and holding the right hand in a protective position. Move the right hand under the left elbow and deliver a right dart fingers thrust. The right bil jee sao retracts and becomes a snake hand, while the left B.D.E.P. changes to a yin knife hand to the neck. Then execute a right B.D.E.P. while turning 30° to the left of centre and moving the left hand into a protective position. Move the left hand under the right elbow and deliver a left dart fingers thrust. The left then becomes a snake hand, while the right changes to a yin knife hand. Continue alternately. See figures 43-46.

43. *B.D.E.P. and palm strike.*
Perform the same movements as described in the previous exercise, but execute a sideward palm strike instead of a yin knife hand. See figure 51.

44. *Jeet sao exercise.*
From basic position execute a left jeet sao and a right protective hand. Then do a right jeet sao and a left protective hand. Do the required number of reps. and sets. See figures 56 and 57.

45. *Shortened arrow punch.*
From basic position execute a left arrow punch while turning 30° to the right of centre. Then retract the left arm slightly and deliver a shortened arrow punch while turning back to basic position. Repeat for required number of reps. Then do the exercise with the right arm for an equal number of times. In all do 3 sets with each arm.

46. *Shortened yin knife hand.*
From basic position execute a left arrow punch while turning 30°to the right of centre. Then retract your left arm slightly, change to a yin knife hand, and immediately deliver a left yin knife hand while turning another 50°. Repeat for required number of reps. Then do the exercise with the right arm for an equal number of times. In all do 3 sets with each arm. See figures 68 and 69.

47. *Monkey hand (fook sao) exercise.*
From the basic I.R.A.S. move the left into a fook sao position. The right remains in fist back position. Turn 30° to the left while executing a circular wrist movement. Return to centre with hand in prayer palm position. Change the left to the monkey hand position and repeat for required number of reps. Then do the movement with the right hand. In all do 3 sets with each arm.

48. *Double snake hand and double vertical palm strike.*
From basic position turn 90° to the left. Then do a double open hand block, save that the forearms are parallel with each other. Move the right foot up so that it is level with the left (keeping knees bent) while changing double tan sao into a double snake hand. Execute a double vertical palm strike. Then revert back to the double open hand block position while moving the right leg back again. Now repeat the sequence for required number of reps. Then reverse positions, i.e., turn to the right for an equal number of reps. Do 3 sets in all.

49. *Double snake hand and double dart fingers thrust.*
Perform the same movements as described in the previous exercise, but execute a double bil jee sao instead of a double vertical palm strike.

50. *Lai sao and sweeping punch.*
From basic position extend arms in preparation for lai sao, right hand closed, left hand open. Turn 90° to right of centre while doing a lai sao. Turn back to centre. The left arm returns to basic fist back position, while the right arm delivers a sweeping punch. The right then delivers a downward palm strike straight forward. Repeat the entire sequence for required number of reps. Then do the exercise for the other side for an equal number of counts. Do 3 sets for each side. See figures 135-140.

51. *Lai sao and front kick.*

From basic position turn 90° to the right while executing a right lai sao. Follow this with a right front kick. Return leg to floor. Turn back to basic position. Repeat for required number of reps. Then turn 90° to the left of centre while executing a left lai sao. Follow this with a left front kick. Turn back to basic position. Repeat for required number of counts. Do 3 sets to each side.

52. *Sliding hand block and cannon punch.*

From basic position move right hand straight in front. Execute a right sliding hand block followed by a right cannon punch. After the required number of reps., repeat the exercise with the left arm. In all do 3 sets to each side. An alternate exercise could be a movement called the "falling star." This consists of the following combinations: sliding hand block, cannon punch to the head and arrow punch to the chest, all with the same arm. This makes a very effective counterattack.

53. *Double elbow punch.*

From basic position, extend both arms straight out, shoulder level, parallel to the floor, palms down. Return the arms back rapidly to the basic position while closing your fists and turning your palms upward. During this exercise concentrate on the elbows. Repeat for required number of reps. and sets.

54. *Semicircular sliding step and sideward palm strike.*

This exercise is based on a wooden dummy movement. Assume the basic I.R.A.S. with the left hand as inquisitive and the right as protective. Take a right semicircular sliding step while executing a right sideward palm strike to the ribs. The left becomes the protective hand. Return to basic position. Then do the exercise for the other side. Repeat alternately for the required number of reps. and sets.

Kicking Exercises for Fourth Day and Fifth Day of Training

Do 3 sets of 20 reps. each side on the exercises.

1. *Alternate knee raises.*

Assume basic I.R.A.S. position. Raise left knee until the thigh is parallel with the floor. Return leg to opening position and then raise the right knee. Continue alternately for 3 sets.

2. *Protective leg.*

Raise your left knee as in the previous exercise, but the toes should be pointed downward. Hold this position for 3 minutes. Then do the same with the right leg. Practice three sessions of 3 minutes with each leg.

3. *Leg snap to side.*

From the basic position raise your right leg, and then snap it down and to the side. Repeat for required number of counts, and then do the same with the left leg. Do 3 sets to each side.

4. *Single-leg horse stance exercise.*
   Raise the left leg. (See Volume II, p.80 for proper position.) Maintain this position for 3 minutes. Continue alternately until you have completed three 3 minute sessions with each leg. You can alternate this exercise with the leg snap to the side.

5. *External rotation block and front kick.*
   From the basic position execute an external rotation block with the left leg followed by a left front kick. Return leg to basic position. Then deliver an external rotation block and front kick with the right leg. Continue alternately for 3 sets with each leg.

6. *Front kick from I.R.A.S.*
   First Set.   Assume I.R.A.S. with right hand as inquisitive and the left as protective. Do a right front kick with the toes up and return to basic position. Then do a left front kick with the toes up while changing the position of the hands. Continue alternately. See figures 176-178.
   Second Set.   Do the front kick with the toes out for the second set.
   Third Set.   Assume I.R.A.S. with left hand as inquisitive and the right as protective. Do a right front kick and a left thrusting block. Return to basic position. Change positions of hands and do a left front kick and a right thrusting block. Continue alternately.

7. *Front kick moving.*
   Execute the front kick while moving forward and backward for required number of reps. and sets. See figures 182-185.

8. *Front kick from a turn.*
   Stand with feet together, 90° to the right. Pivot so that you are 30° to the right of centre. Deliver a kick to the front. Then assume the basic I.R.A.S. Return to original position and repeat the cycle for the required number of counts. Do the same with the right leg an equal number of times. Complete 3 sets with each leg.

9. *Hammer kick.*
   Complete 3 sets with each leg of the hammer kick exercise. See figures 186-188.

10. *Front Kick and Side Kick while pivoting.*
    Assume a basic on guard position, left hand inquisitive and right hand protective. Execute a left front kick. Then deliver a left side kick while pivoting on the right leg. Return to original position. Repeat for required number of reps. Then do the same with the right leg. In all do 3 sets with each leg. See figures 191 and 192.

11. *Side kick exercise number one.*
    Stand with feet together 90° to the left. Execute a side kick to the level of an opponent's stomach or ribs. Repeat for the required number of counts. Then do the same with the left leg for an equal number of reps. In all do 3 sets for each leg.

12. *Side kick exercise number two.*
From the basic position, execute a left front kick. Then immediately perform a side kick to the ankle of an imaginary opponent. Without returning your leg to the ground, deliver another left front kick. Return to basic position. Then repeat the cycle with the right leg. Continue alternately for 3 sets with each leg.

13. *T'o kick combination.*
Imagine an opponent facing you with his right leg advanced. From basic I.R.A.S. execute a right t'o movement knocking the imaginary opponent off balance by kicking his right foot. Then execute with a right side kick to the left (supporting) leg of the opponent. Follow up with a right stamping kick to the knee of your imaginary opponent. Continue for required number of reps. Then repeat the combination with the left leg. In all do 3 sets with each leg.

14. *Front kick with a double snake hand from a charging stance.*
Do 3 sets with each leg. See figures 179 and 180.

15. *Alternate side kicks with a pivot.*
Do 3 sets with each leg.

16. *Side kicks with a pivot.*
Do 3 sets with each leg.

17. *Low wing and side kick.*
Do 3 sets with each leg.

18. *Side kick while jumping.*
Do 3 sets with each leg. See figures 193-195.

19. *Front kick, wing hand, and stamping kick.*
Assume basic I.R.A.S. with the right hand as inquisitive and the left as protective. Deliver a right front kick. Then pivot on your left foot slightly while doing a right wing hand and a right stamping kick to the knee of an imaginary opponent. Return to basic position. Change the positions of your hands, and repeat the combination with the left leg. Continue alternately for 3 sets with each leg. This exercise is similar to a wooden dummy technique.

20. *Jeet sao and side kick.*
Assume basic I.R.A.S. with the right hand as inquisitive and the left as protective. Pivot slightly on your left foot while executing a right jeet sao and delivering a right side kick to the ribs of an imaginary opponent. Return to basic position. Change the positions of your hands, and repeat the sequence on the other side. Continue alternately for 3 sets.

Suggested Training Schedule.

First Day.
Wooden dummy techniques followed by the Sil Lim Tao Set.

Second Day.
The Chum Kil Set, exercises 1-27, and sparring (especially sticking hands from levels one and two).

Third Day.
The Bil Jee Set, exercises 28-54, and sparring (sticking hands).

Fourth Day.
Kicking exercises 1-10, and sparring for kicks as described in level two.

Fifth Day.
Kicking exercises 11-20, and sparring for kicks.

Concluding Remarks
   Various sparring routines can be selected from the three levels, but do not neglect sticking hands, which should be practiced while blindfolded. Make use of sandbags in your training. Be sure to fill the sandbags with fine sand, but do not fill them completely because there must be a give when you punch in order to execute the punch with a snap. A sandbag can be used also like a medicine ball, i.e., tossed back and forth. Once a week check the force of your punches by taking the candle test. You should practice empty and solid hitting in your training. Empty punching involves striking the air. This is very important for speed and form. But at least one third of your training should be devoted to solid hitting against a sandbag mounted on the wall. For variety you can try striking paper, a handkerchief, or a string hanging from the ceiling. The use of string is especially effective. It becomes the centreline. You punch, strike, and kick at it without touching it. You can attach a ball to a string suspended from the ceiling. Have a person push the ball while you practice various palm strikes. Sandbags can be used to practice various types of kicks too. In addition, a wooden stake or several of them can be buried in the ground in order to practice kicks and to develop power. Good luck in your training. Be patient, and do not be discouraged. We wish to concluded by repeating again the words of Spinoza: "All things excellent are as difficult as they are rare."

BIL JEE SET

1

2

3

Figs. 1-4. Enter the horse stance.
Fig. 1. Legs straight, feet together, fists back.
Fig. 2. Quarter squat.
Fig. 3. Semicircular sliding step with left leg.
Fig. 4. Semicircular sliding step with right leg.
Now in I.R.A.S.
Figs. 5-13. Sequence beginning with left arrow punch and wrist movements.
Fig. 5. Left arrow punch.
Fig. 6. Open fist to form leaf palm.

4

5

6

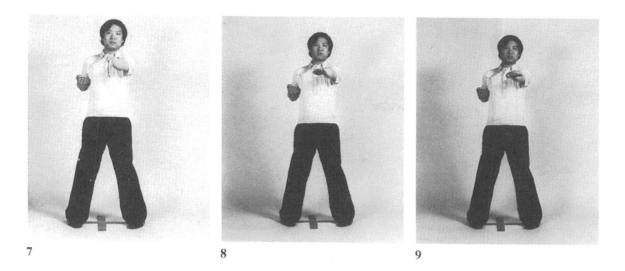

7   8   9

Fig. 7. Move hand downward by ulnar deviation. Return hand to position in figure 6 and repeat two more times, i.e. the movement is executed three times.

Fig. 8. Move hand so that the palm is down.

Fig. 9. Move hand to left by a radial deviation. Return hand to position in figure 8 and repeat two more times, i.e., the movement is executed three times.

Figs. 10-13. Circular wrist and return to I.R.A.S.

10   11   12

13   14   15

Figs. 14-22. Sequence beginning with right arrow punch.

Fig. 14. Right arrow punch.

Fig. 15. Open fist to form leaf palm.

Fig. 16. Move hand downward by ulnar deviation. Return hand to position in figure 15 and repeat two more times, i.e., the movement is executed three times.

Fig. 17. Move hand so that the palm is down.

Fig. 18. Move hand to right by radial deviation. Return hand to position in figure 17 and repeat two more times, i.e., the movement is executed three times.

16   17   18

106

19

20

21

Figs. 19-22. Circular wrist and return to I.R.A.S.
Figs. 23-34. Left B.D.E.P. and bil jee sao sequence.
Fig. 23. Left B.D.E.P. while turning 90° to the right of centre.
Fig. 24. Right B.D.E.P. while turning 90° to left of centre.

22

23

24

25 **26** **27**

Fig. 25. Left B.D.E.P. while turning 90° to the right of centre.
Fig. 26. Right hand brought under elbow of left B.D.E.P.
Fig. 27. Right dart fingers thrust (bil jee sao).
Fig. 28. Left bil jee sao while bringing left foot up even with right, feet together.
Figs. 29-32. Circular wrist to fist back position.

28 **29** **30**

31

32

33

Figs. 33-34. Semicircular sliding step with left leg and return to I.R.A.S. as in figure 22.
Figs. 35-46. Right B.D.E.P. and bil jee sao sequence.
Fig. 35. Right B.D.E.P. while turning 90° to left of centre.
Fig. 36. Left B.D.E.P. while turning 90° to right of centre.

34

35

36

37

38

39

Fig. 37. Right B.D.E.P. while turning 90° to left of centre.
Fig. 38. Left hand brought under elbow of right B.D.E.P.
Fig. 39. Left dart fingers thrust (bil jee sao).
Fig. 40. Right bil jee sao while bringing right foot up even with left, feet together.

Fig. 41-44. Circular wrist to fist back position.

40

41

42

43

44

45

Figs. 45-46. Semicircular sliding step with right leg and return to I.R.A.S. as in figures 22 and 34.

Figs. 47-60. Left B.D.E.P. and yin knife hand to rib area sequence.

Fig. 47. Left B.D.E.P. while turning 90° to right of centre.

Fig. 48. Right B.D.E.P. while turning 90° to left of centre.

46

47

48

49   **50**   **51**

Fig. 49. Left B.D.E.P. while turning 90° to right of centre.

Fig. 50. Right hand brought under elbow of left B.D.E.P.

Fig. 51. Right bil jee sao.

Fig. 52. Left yin knife hand to rib area while right returns to basic fist back position.

Fig. 53. Left jeet sao while returning to basic position facing front. Right remains in fist back position.

Fig. 54. Left push down palm.

52   **53**   **54**

55

56

57

Fig. 55. Left still extended but changed to position for a diagonal sweep and chop. Right moves into position by left elbow for diagonal sweep and chop.

Fig. 56. Right has completed diagonal sweep and chop, and left is brought back to basic fist back position.

Figs. 57-60. Circular wrist and return to I.R.A.S. *Note* that not all of the hand movements are always pictured for the circular wrist. Turn the palm up to begin circular wrist.

58

59

60

61   62   63

Fig. 61-74. Right B.D.E.P. and yin knife hand to rib area sequence.
Fig. 61. Right B.D.E.P. while turning 90° to left of centre.
Fig. 62. Left B.D.E.P. while turning 90° to right of centre.
Fig. 63. Right B.D.E.P. while turning 90° to left of centre.
Fig. 64. Left hand brought under elbow of right B.D.E.P.
Fig. 65. Left bil jee sao.
Fig. 66. Right yin knife hand to rib area while left returns to basic fist back position.

64   65   66

67   68   69

Fig. 67. Right jeet sao while returning to basic position facing front. Left remains in fist back position.

Fig. 68. Right push down palm.

Fig. 69. Right still extended but changed to position for diagonal sweep and chop. Left moves into position by right elbow for diagonal sweep and chop.

Fig. 70. Left has completed diagonal sweep and chop, and right is brought back to basic fist back position.

Figs. 71-74. Circular wrist and return to I.R.A.S.

70   71   72

73   74   75

Figs. 75-88. Left B.D.E.P. and yin knife hand to neck area sequence.
Fig. 75. Left B.D.E.P. while turning 90° to right of centre.
Fig. 76. Right B.D.E.P. while turning 90° to left of centre.
Fig. 77. Left B.D.E.P. while turning 90° to right of centre.
Fig. 78. Right hand brought under elbow of left B.D.E.P.

76   77   78

79

80

81

Fig. 79. Right bil jee sao.
Fig. 80. Left yin knife hand to neck area while right returns to basic fist back position.
Fig. 81. Left jeet sao while returning to basic position facing front. Right remains in fist back position.
Fig. 82. Left push down palm.

Fig. 83. Left still extended but changed to position for a diagonal sweep and chop. Right moves into position by left elbow for diagonal sweep and chop.
Fig. 84. Right has completed diagonal sweep and chop and left is brought back to basic fist back position.

82

83

84

85

86

87

Figs. 85-88. Circular wrist and return to   of centre.
I.R.A.S.
Figs. 89-102. Right B.D.E.P. and yin knife
hand to neck area sequence.
Fig. 89. Right B.D.E.P. while turning 90° to left
of centre.
Fig. 90. Left B.D.E.P. while turning 90° to right

88

89

90

91

92

93

Fig. 91. Right B.D.E.P. while turning 90° to left of centre.
Fig. 92. Left hand brought under elbow of right B.D.E.P.
Fig. 93. Left bil jee sao.
Fig. 94. Right yin knife hand to neck area while left returns to basic fist back position.

Fig. 95. Right jeet sao while returning to basic position facing front. Left remains in fist back position.
Fig. 96. Right push down palm.

94

95

96

97 **98** **99**

Fig. 97. Right still extended but changed to position for a diagonal sweep and chop. Left moves into position by right elbow for a diagonal sweep and chop.
Fig. 98. Left has completed diagonal sweep and chop and right is brought back to basic fist back position.

Figs. 99-102. Circular wrist and return to I.R.A.S.

100 **101** **102**

103   104   105

Figs. 103-115. Sequence beginning with left jeet sao.
Fig. 103. Left jeet sao, right protective hand.
Fig. 104. Right jeet sao, left protective hand.
Fig. 105. Left jeet sao, right protective hand.
Fig. 106. Left push down palm while right returns to basic fist back position.

Fig. 107. Beginning of left circular wrist.
Fig. 108. Continuation of left circular wrist while turning 30° to left of centre.

106   107   108

109 **110** **111**

Fig. 109. Turn back to centre while changing to left prayer palm. Repeat movements illustrated in figures 107-109 twice more.

Figs. 110. Then left prayer palm changes to position for a diagonal sweep and chop. Right moves into position by left elbow for diagonal sweep and chop.

Fig. 111. Right has completed diagonal sweep and chop, and left is brought back to basic fist back position.

Figs. 112-115. Circular wrist and return to I.R.A.S.

112 **113** **114**

115

116

117

Figs. 116-128. Sequence beginning with right jeet sao.
Fig. 116. Right jeet sao, left protective hand.
Fig. 117. Left jeet sao, right protective hand.
Fig. 118. Right jeet sao, left protective hand.
Fig. 119. Right push down palm while left returns to basic fist back position.

Fig. 120. Beginning of right circular wrist.

118

119

120

123

121

122

123

Fig. 121. Continuation of right circular wrist while turning 30° to right of centre.

Fig. 122. Turn back to centre while changing to right prayer palm. Repeat movements illustrated in figures 120-122 twice more.

Fig. 123. Then right prayer palm changes to position for a diagonal sweep and chop. Left moves into position by right elbow for diagonal sweep and chop.

Fig. 124. Left has completed diagonal sweep and chop, and right is brought back to fist back position.

Figs. 125-128. Circular wrist and return to I.R.A.S.

124

125

126

127

128

129

Figs. 129-142. Sequence beginning with left bil jee sao.
Fig. 129. Left bil jee sao.
Fig. 130. Bring right hand under elbow of left arm.
Fig. 131. Execute a right bil jee sao and retract left hand to a position under the elbow of the right arm.
Fig. 132. Left bil jee sao while right returns to basic fist back position.

130

131

132

133

134

135

Fig. 133. Left yin knife hand to neck area while turning 90° to right of centre.
Fig. 134. Left jeet sao while returning to basic position facing front.
Fig. 135. Left push down palm.
Fig. 136. Left still extended but changed to position for a diagonal sweep and chop. Right

moves into position by left elbow for diagonal sweep and chop.
Fig. 137. Right has completed diagonal sweep and chop, and left is brought back to basic fist back position.
Figs. 138-142. Circular wrist and return to I.R.A.S.

136

137

138

139 **140** **141**

Figs. 143-156. Sequence beginning with right bil
jee sao.
Fig. 143. Right bil jee sao.
Fig. 144. Bring left hand under elbow of right
arm.

142 **143** **144**

145

146

147

Fig. 145. Execute a left bil jee sao and retract right hand to a position under the elbow of the left arm.

Fig. 146. Right bil jee sao while left returns to basic fist back position.

Fig. 147. Right yin knife hand to neck area while turning 90° to left of centre.

Fig. 148. Right jeet sao while returning to basic position facing front.

Fig. 149. Right push down palm.

Fig. 150. Right still extended but changed to position for a diagonal sweep and chop. Left moves into position by right elbow for diagonal sweep and chop.

148

149

150

151

152

153

Fig. 151. Left has completed diagonal sweep and chop, and right is brought back to basic fist back position.
Figs. 152-156. Circular wrist and return to I.R.A.S.

154

155

156

157

158

159

Figs. 157-165. Sequence beginning with right cultivating hand.

Fig. 157. Right cultivating hand and left yin knife hand while turning 30° to right of centre.

Fig. 158. Left cultivating hand and right yin knife hand while turning 30° to left of centre.

Fig. 159. Turn back to centre while executing a left drop elbow block. Right returns to basic fist back position.

Fig. 160. Left moves into position for diagonal sweep and chop. Right is also in place by left elbow for diagonal sweep and chop.

Fig. 161. Right has completed diagonal sweep and chop, and left is brought back to basic fist back position.

160

161

162

163

164

165

Figs. 162-165. Circular wrist and return to I.R.A.S. Note that you should turn palm up as in figure 138 to begin circular wrist.

Figs. 166-175. Sequence beginning with left cultivating hand.

Fig. 166. Left cultivating hand and right yin knife hand while turning 30° to the left of centre.

Fig. 167. Right cultivating hand and left yin knife hand while turning 30° to the right of centre.

Fig. 168. Turn back to centre while executing a right drop elbow block. Left returns to basic fist back position.

166

167

168

169   **170**   **171**

Fig. 169. Right moves into position for a diagonal sweep and chop. Left is also in place by right elbow for diagonal sweep and chop.
Fig. 170. Left has completed diagonal sweep and chop, and right is brought back to basic fist back position.
Figs. 171-175. Circular wrist and return to

I.R.A.S.

172   **173**   **174**

175

176

177

Figs. 176-183. Sequence beginning with lai sao to right.
Fig. 176. Extend arms in preparation for lai sao, right hand closed, left hand open.
Fig. 177. Turn 90° to right of centre while doing a lai sao.
Fig. 178. Turn back to centre. The left arm returns to basic fist back position, while the right arm delivers a sweeping punch.
Fig. 179. Right delivers a downward palm strike straight forward.
Figs. 180-183. Circular wrist and return to I.R.A.S. Note that circular wrist begins with palm up.

178

179

180

181

182

183

Figs. 184-191. Sequence beginning with lai sao to left.

Fig. 184. Extend arms in preparation for lai sao, left hand closed, right hand open.

Fig. 185. Turn 90° to left of centre while doing a lai sao.

Fig. 186. Turn back to centre. The right arm returns to basic fist back position, while the left arm delivers a sweeping punch.

184

185

186

187
188
189

Fig. 187. Left delivers a downward palm strike straight forward.
Figs. 188-191. Circular wrist and return to I.R.A.S.
Fig. 192. Bend over as shown.

190
191
192

193   **194**

Fig. 193. Execute a right front kick while
moving hands into guarding position as shown.
Fig. 194. Return to I.R.A.S.